D1010858

A World of Ways

to Say "I Do"

Wedding Vows, Readings, Poems, and Customs

from Different Traditions and Cultures

NOAH BENSHEA & JORDAN BENSHEA

McGraw·Hill

New York   Chicago   San Francisco   Lisbon   London   Madrid   Mexico City
Milan   New Delhi   San Juan   Seoul   Singapore   Sydney   Toronto

The **McGraw·Hill** Companies

Library of Congress Cataloging-in-Publication Data

BenShea, Noah.
    A world of ways to say "I do" : wedding vows, readings, poems, and customs
from different traditions and cultures / Noah benShea and Jordan benShea.
        p.   cm.
    ISBN 0-07-142295-1 (alk. paper)
    1. Marriage service.   I. BenShea, Jordan.   II. Title.

    BL619.M37B47   2004
    392.5—dc22   2003027540

1 2 3 4 5 6 7 8 9 0   FGR/FGR   3 2 1 0 9 8 7 6 5 4

ISBN 0-07-142295-1

Interior design by Steve Straus

McGraw-Hill books are available at special quantity discounts to use as premiums
and sales promotions, or for use in corporate training programs. For more
information, please write to the Director of Special Sales, Professional Publishing,
McGraw-Hill, Two Penn Plaza, New York, NY 10121-2298. Or contact your local
bookstore.

This book is printed on acid-free paper.

This book is dedicated to love and laughter.

Contents

Contents

Give Her a Smooch

A life insurance company did a study and found that men who kiss their wives each morning before they leave for work:

- *live an average of five years longer*
- *are involved in fewer auto accidents*
- *are ill 50 percent less time*
- *earn 20 to 30 percent more money*

P.S. Wives whose husbands kiss them each morning, kiss back.

Introduction
Congratulations!

Where there is love there is life.
— MAHATMA GANDHI

Congratulations! Welcome to love and marriage. Like the ring you are about to wear, you are joining a timeless circle—a circle that unites lovers around the world. And now that you're planning your wedding, this is a good time to take a deep breath and pause for a moment to reflect on all the love and happiness that has brought you to this place and moment in time.

Our first word of advice is . . . relax. Life is not a dress rehearsal, and your wedding should not be a stress-rehearsal. Getting married is supposed to be one of the best experiences in a person's life, yet very often there is too much anxiety and expectation about the marriage ceremony and too little joy in the process. The words you use to say "I do" say much about what you expect from your marriage, which is why it's very important that your vows reflect your individual love.

Wedding vows should not be seen as lines that you've been handed and told to memorize and recite. Vows of love are agreements of the heart that you can—and should—have a hand in creating. Getting married is more than a play where you are told where to stand and what to say, and creating your wedding vows is very important in giving your hand in marriage and taking someone's for life. With your vows, you have the opportunity to share your deepest feelings of devotion, loyalty, and pure love. They are more than words. Wedding vows are magic because they turn a man and woman into a husband and wife.

In these pages, we hope you will find a wise and gentle friend who will offer ideas and inspiration so you can incorporate meaningful words and thoughts of love into your special day. Here you will discover how others from around the world and across time have chosen to say "I do," as well as some thinking on how to add in thoughts from many cultures and religions. Some couples choose vows that are tried and true. Others want to pledge a traditional commitment while expressing their uniqueness. If you want to make your vows special, we vow to help you.

This book is meant to be more than simply a guide to writing wedding vows. You'll also discover ideas and customs from around the world that you can learn or borrow from in many ways to add meaning to your special day. You will find quotations on love and marriage that might make you think or laugh, or might simply touch your heart. You can draw on these brief insights for your readings, programs, or other aspects of your wedding. You can also use them in notes to your friends, on your wedding website, or perhaps just share them with your partner during those moments when a wise thought or a wry laugh will help remind you of what's really important. The rich array of expression in this book can help you articulate your thoughts and describe your unique love.

In the following chapters you will occasionally see the word *adapted* following a poem or vow. This means that we have adapted the language or length to reflect how the quotation spoke to our hearts or we felt would best serve you. You should not hesitate to do the same. As you work on your vows and draw on the rich resources in this book, freely edit passages and put thoughts in your own words.

When you get married, you enter into a wonderful new world of commitment based on love, mutual trust, and friendship. For some, finding the right person and falling in love is less difficult than finding the words to express how we feel. We wrote this book to give you a world's worth of wisdom on love and marriage, so that you can ponder the universality of love as well as learn new insights from ancient cultures.

Our aim is to make this "world of ways" your banquet. On this buffet table you will be able to pick and choose, mix and match, and, most important, find your own feast. Our thought in writing this book was never to tell you what to do, but to offer you a broad range of options to help you make your vows timely, timeless, and creative. Here you can borrow from the past, be in the present, and prepare for the future.

The sharing of vows should be an extraordinary experience for both of you, but one sure way to get lost during this adventure is to forget to keep in touch with each other. You and your partner need to be each other's "magnetic north." If you stay in close touch with each other, even in the middle of all the planning and madness, you will find your way together.

Oh yes, and don't forget to laugh, often. If only because getting married is not a laughing matter. Little causes more heartbreak and heartburn during the prewedding buzz than lovers who lose their sense of humor. Laugh at what doesn't work. Laugh at yourself for confusing the caterer's commitment with your commitment to each other. Even old tensions can make for great humor. During this time, worry less about being right and more about how right you are for each other.

Now that you are about to make a vow of love, remember that this might be the most important promise you will ever make. If you doubt this, ask anyone who has broken that promise or had his or her heart broken. So whether this is the first time you have walked down the aisle, or you have been fortunate to find the faith to fall in love again, whether you are a grown-up or growing up, whether you and your lover come from the same background or are just grateful to find someone special in your foreground, here is *A World of Ways to Say "I Do."*

We think one more element adds something special to the cornucopia of thoughts and traditions on marriage found in these pages. While this book has a shared authorship, the authors share more—we are father and daughter. As father and daughter, we like to think we bring both experience and youthful exuberance to this project, which you can use to help you sail through the wedding planning process with both your sanity and sense of humor fully intact.

The idea of doing a father and daughter book on wedding vows came about because we realized that, while all who attend the wedding ceremony are there to honor the love of the bride and groom, few draw as much meaning from the ceremony as a father and daughter. Fathers and daughters can be very close and very different, and we are both. One is more traditional and pretty religious. (Yes, that's the father.) And the other is more contemporary and more spiritual than religious. (Yes, that's the daughter.) We brought together these two different perspectives to serve you, as a twin-ply rope is stronger for the weaving of the two strands.

A father generally wants his daughter to share in his sense of tradition. A daughter wants to respect this but also wants to embrace what is timely as well as what is time-less. Together, we've learned that being right is less important than having our hearts in the right place and helping each other find the right way. To that end, we've tried to bring some of that life-caring and life-sharing into this book. We hope that you will find not only tradition and insight, but also acceptance on these pages, because when you and your partner exchange vows you will also exchange mutual acceptance of each other's lives, history, background, and beliefs.

Imagine your vows as your work of art and yourself as the artist. We are the artist's servants. In this book, our work is to lay out the colors on the palette, prepare the brushes and canvas, and remind you that you'll do a great job on your work of art.

Although we don't know you, we do know that we want the very best for you on your wedding day. Father and daughter, one generation to the next, we wish you the best. You deserve no less. We hope you're smiling and can feel us smiling back.

Save us a bite of the wedding cake—and may your wedding be a piece of cake.

Writing Your Own Wedding Vows

The tongue is the pen of the heart.
—YIDDISH PROVERB

*I*n almost every tradition the vows state that you take each other for richer or for poorer and in sickness and in health. During a glittering ceremony, a recent bride who was much younger than her very, very wealthy groom paused in reflection after the minister prompted, "for richer or poorer" and said, "Well . . ." and got a big laugh from the audience.

Your wedding vows—how you say them and what you say—will be the most individual and unique part of your ceremony. No matter which words you choose, speak from your heart and to your partner's. Think of your vows as a heartwarming and heart-to-heart conversation between the two of you, but this time with people listening in and cheering you on.

Sometimes it takes someone else to say exactly what we're thinking. So whether your marriage is a celebration of differences, a celebration of different generations, or whether you've been down the aisle before, here you might find quotes to remind you or others how you feel in choosing your partner. Perhaps one or two of these quotes might find a way into your vows as a way to share what you're feeling with your family and friends.

This chapter on crafting your own vows shouldn't take away from the traditional vows that are offered as resources in Chapter 3. In fact, with so much change going on in the world, sometimes being traditional can be pretty original. Whether you wish to write your own vows from scratch or are looking to supplement more traditional vows, the advice in this chapter may be useful to you.

While this is your wedding, you are also marching up the aisle of other people's expectations. And in some religions and traditions how much you can add to or modify the traditional needs to be considered. You should check with whoever is going to marry you well in advance of the ceremony to make sure you're all on the same page.

If your heart is about to burst forth in song or sonnets about how good life is, the following suggestions will help you organize your bliss and express your feelings in a way that won't make you blush when watching your video after the wedding. You are the right person to write your own vows. You don't have to be Shakespeare to do this. In fact, the hardest part for most people is getting over the first hurdle: starting. The best way to accomplish any daunting task is to take the first step. This next section will show you how.

Simple Steps for Writing Your Wedding Vows

Here are a few simple steps that will help you write your wedding vows. As with so many journeys in life, this one never requires you to take more than one step at a time.

Step 1: Decide Whether to Write Your Vows Together or Separately

The first decision you and your partner need to make is whether you want to write your vows together or work on them individually. Either way, you will wind up working together, so you should base your decision simply on whether you feel most comfortable and creative doing it together or apart. For some couples, the exercise of writing vows together can be among the first real challenges in the relationship. For others, the process can be a joyful sharing time during which the bride and groom recall why they're undertaking this task in the first place. Whether you begin together or apart, be assured there is no right or wrong way, there are only differences in what you may get out of doing it one way or the other.

With all the noise and pressure of planning a wedding, working apart on your vows might give you some breathing room as well as some perspective on your own thoughts and feelings. It also might allow for more honesty and creativity because you won't have the pressure of trying to match what your fiancé is writing. Use this time to relax, breathe deeply, and meditate on how you met, how you felt falling in love, and how you envision the rest of your lives together. Appreciate this monumental time.

If you choose to begin by working together, you might find that you can craft vows that have some measure of continuity and similarity in structure. You have the opportunity to discuss how personal you want to get and whether you want to speak the same vows, slightly different versions, or ones that are unique to your own thoughts and feelings. What feels best to you? Do you want a more structured ceremony, or do you like the free-spirited feeling of speaking different vows? Set the stage and use this time to appreciate one another. Maybe even dish up a romantic meal, pour a couple of glasses of wine, light the candles, and let the evening unfold as a process and a tribute to your love for one another.

Step 2: Create a List of Meaningful Words and Phrases

Next, make a comprehensive list of meaningful words and phrases. These can be feelings and emotions, nouns and verbs, song lyrics and phrases from poems, activities you've done together, even your pet names. It might help to think of moments you've shared and identify the words to describe those times and the emotions inspired by them. For example, think about:

- *An adventure you had together*
- *The lyrics of "your" song or the song you'll have your first dance to*
- *The most romantic movie you ever saw and dialogue from it*

- A *poem you have read or a poem your love has quoted to you or composed for you*
- *Your love letters to each other*
- *Famous quotes that have been particularly meaningful to you*
- *How you would describe your partner if you were writing to a friend you haven't been in touch with for a while*
- *A tough time or a period of doubt that you went through and how you survived it with your partner's help*
- *The first time you saw him or her, the first time you held hands, or your first kiss and how it made you feel*
- *The first time you professed your love for one another*
- *What it will be like to grow older together*
- *What you have in common, as well as your differences*
- *Which character traits you would most want your children (if you plan to have any) to inherit from your future husband or wife*

In no particular order, without too much thought or planning, write down words that describe the main themes of your lives together. Once you have a fairly long list, rank them in order of importance or place a check mark next to words or phrases that are especially significant to you.

This exercise can be particularly interesting when you undertake it separately. But even if you're working together, sit down with separate sheets of paper and pens and give yourselves twenty minutes to complete your lists. At the end of the allowed time, compare and contrast them. See which words or phrases, feelings or memories your lists have in common.

Now that you've got something down about how you feel, you've got a great beginning!

Step 3: Explore Traditional Wedding Vows

Sometimes it's difficult to write something so important without a framework with which to begin. So take some time to review Chapter 3 to see the structure and word choice used in vows from a variety of cultures and religions. Pay particular attention to those that are traditional to your backgrounds or simply read them all and flag those that somehow speak to you.

Make notes of the parts you find most meaningful. Then put them into your own words, or take the language in the traditional vows and put it alongside the words you and your beloved have written. As long as you are speaking from your heart, feel free to open yourselves up to what others have said that reflects what you want to say.

Step 4: Decide the Length of Your Vows

Because men are generally less inclined to speak of their emotions in public, for them writing vows might be an exercise in saying as much as possible in as few words as possible. Conversely, women are generally more comfortable expressing their feelings, so a woman could spend the afternoon making her vows a stream-of-consciousness monologue lasting several hours.

Regardless of whether your relationship follows this pattern, or whether you're both verbal or both taciturn, in this step you must decide together how long you want your vows to be. To that end, you might have specific suggestions from your officiant, and keep in mind the total length of the ceremony. How many songs and readings will you have? If the service is primarily religious, how long will that part of the ceremony take? Be considerate of your guests and know that they might be sitting and standing for some time.

Whether you choose to keep it brief or want to be comprehensive in your vows, it's difficult to judge the actual length in speaking time until you've written your vows and timed yourself speaking them out loud. You can always edit down or add more, but you should have an idea as you proceed of their approximate length.

Step 5: Write Your Vows

Now that you have a comprehensive list of meaningful words, ideas, feelings, and phrases, it's time to put them in some kind of order. Think about what you want the focus of your vows to be. Do you want to speak to the institution of marriage, including its symbols and meaning? Do you want to focus on your love and commitment to each other? Or do you want to combine aspects of both?

Above all, don't worry about trying to make this into a polished draft with correct spelling and perfect prose. Your goal should be to simply write down your feelings as accurately as possible. Don't write what you think others expect of you or what you think everyone is supposed to say at a wedding . . . unless that is what you want to say. The magic word here is *honesty*, which means speaking with feeling and trust, and trusting yourself. After all, love has a language of its own, and your goal should be to discover the words to describe yours.

Think of your vows in terms of writing a story: what will be the beginning, the middle, and the end? As with all good stories, rough drafts must be written and revised — sometimes multiple times. Read what you've written and think about the word choices you've made, whether they most effectively express and describe how you feel. Say them out loud. How do they sound? Do they flow together in a pleasing way?

Finally, once you have a rough draft, time yourselves, speaking your vows slowly. Your vows should be approximately equal in terms of length so they don't seem imbalanced. But the final rule is always go with what feels right to you.

Step 6: Share Time

Odds are that by this time each of you is in love with what you wrote, and you're probably fairly pleased and proud of your accomplishment—and you should be! If you've written your vows separately, now is the time to get together and share what you've written. As you each listen to what the other has written, make a commitment to not be judgmental. As you share, be sure to listen to your own vows as if for the first time, with an open heart and an open mind.

The key word during this time of wedding planning and vow writing is *compromise*. Too many people confuse compromise as selling out or losing self. In reality, compromise is a way to avoid becoming lost in ourselves. No relationship survives without it, and steadfast marriages are built on solid foundations of compromise, caring, and consideration.

When you read what your love has written, don't cross out words, correct misspellings, or make changes. Instead, take this time to point out what you like the most, what touches your heart and resonates with you, or what rings your bell. With caring and consideration, combine the best of what the two of you have written to create vows that truly reflect the merging of your hearts and minds.

Once you and your partner are satisfied with the vows that have been created, share them with the person who is going to perform your ceremony. His or her experience with weddings and knowledge of both of you will provide some valuable insight and suggestions. In the end it's your call, but take advantage of the wisdom of those you respect and who have done this before.

The Final Step

Take your vows out for a test drive. With the draft copy in one hand and your beloved's hand in the other, read through your vows together, slowly. When you feel your heart pitter-patter and your eyes grow moist, you'll know that you've created meaningful words to bind you together in joy for a lifetime. And there you have it—the vows you never thought you could write.

Make Your Vows Accessible to All

As you move forward in final edits of your vows, keep in mind and close to your heart that a marriage links you to the past, present, and the future and that you should speak to all three in your vows. In addition, the following guidelines might prove useful in guiding the final crafting of your vows:

- *Unless the two of you are getting married by yourselves, remember that many others will be sharing this day with you. Don't make your vows so personal they will be baffling to those witnessing the event. Make your vows a blend of private thoughts available to the public.*

- *You've invited friends and family to your wedding, so why not invite them into the vows? Let your family and friends know how you count on them to support you and what they mean to you, perhaps even in a brief mention during your vows.*

- *While the purpose of your vows is not to entertain your audience, likewise, they don't have to be dull and lifeless. Think of your vows as the knockout punch of the wedding ceremony, so pack a lot of feeling into them.*

Need More Direction?

Don't just write about loving him or her forever, but loving him when he forgets to take out the trash or loving her when she moves the remote. Write about how he loves you no matter how many times you tell him to take out the trash or about how she loves you no matter how often you go ballistic looking for the remote. Don't be afraid to get personal in your vows. After all, there's no occasion more personal than a wedding!

Don't worry if you feel that what you most want to tell your bride or groom in your vows seems trite. The truth often seems trite at first glance. In fact, however, saying, "I love you with all my heart" is never trite, it's timeless.

Because we are a media generation, an alternate, and perhaps easier, method of crafting your vows is to think of writing what you are feeling in dialogue. Think of your vows as a back-and-forth conversation during which you profess your commitment to each other. For example:

HE: *I hand you my fears and my strengths. I give you what I would never allow anyone else to take.*

SHE: *I accept your fears and strengths and hand you my fears and my strengths, and I give you what I would never allow anyone else to take.*

SHE: *I give you love that is more than passion. I give you intimacy and I ask you to guard it.*

HE: *I will guard your intimacy, and I give you love that is more than passion. I give you a love that is beyond reason but gives me a reason to live.*

The single biggest tip for writing your wedding vows is, once again, Don't lose your sense of humor. Nothing serves romance like laughter. Write about what he or she does that makes you laugh, and how the sound of your beloved's laughter makes your heart giggle. When his blue eyes fade, his laughter will still keep you warm at night. When her hair has gone gray, her willingness to hear your jokes one more time will remind you she's the right one.

For Couples from Different Religious Backgrounds

If yours is an interfaith marriage—congratulations! As it says in the old gospel song, "All God's children got wings." Interfaith weddings are a beautiful time to embrace your and your loved one's beliefs in a way that is respectful to both of you and to the decisions you have made on how faith and cultural heritage will play into your marriage. Your wedding ceremony is an opportunity to bring together your core values and beliefs with vows and readings that reflect those decisions.

At the beginning of the wedding process have a discussion—first with your fiancé and then with your family—to get everyone's views on faith and what each person desires from the ceremony. Let your families know that you want to hear their opinions. Sit down with them and ask what part of their religion they wish could be highlighted in the ceremony. Then take some time and ask yourselves the same question. You should candidly discuss how you want your wedding ceremony and vows to be structured. Think about the specific elements of your faiths that are important to each of you and what aspects complement the other's faith.

When you meet with the person who will marry you, ask for his or her opinion about the structure and content of the wedding. Perhaps your officiant will offer insight into ways to honor the different perspectives without losing your integrity and decision. In the end you will no doubt receive a lot of different opinions, but ultimately you will decide how you wish to conduct the ceremony.

After you've had a chance to think and find where you are on this, gather your families and explain your decisions in a manner that is respectful to you and them. The most important thing throughout this process is that you are honest with your feelings and openly discuss the significance of your decisions and your faiths with the respect they deserve.

You can also achieve harmony by sitting down as a couple and making a list of traditions or religious practices that may need to be explained to those in attendance at the ceremony. If the ceremony is in a language different from what is spoken by many of your guests, consider providing translations to make sure everyone feels included.

Additionally, you might want to spend some time browsing through readings and poems that reflect your religious beliefs and can be used in your ceremony. Either follow the tradition of your religion carefully or be a bit more creative. Whatever you decide, it is imperative that both of you feel respected and are able to communicate your faiths equally in the ceremony.

Pose the following questions to yourself and to your future spouse as you prepare to write your vows:

- *What do I most value about my religious upbringing?*
- *What do I value in the customs and traditions of my partner's religious heritage?*
- *What do we share in common?*

- *What difficulties have we overcome, and what have they taught us?*
- *How does my love enrich my faith?*

Quotations Celebrating Difference

The diversity of the phenomena of nature is so great, and the treasures hidden in the heavens so rich, precisely in order that the human mind shall never be lacking in fresh nourishment.

—JOHANNES KEPLER

One's life has value so long as one attributes value to the life of others.

—SIMONE DE BEAUVOIR

It is in the shelter of each other that the people live.

—IRISH PROVERB

Everyone needs to be valued. Everyone has the potential to give something back.

—DIANA, PRINCESS OF WALES

*If we cannot now end our differences, at least we
can help make the world safe for diversity.*

—JOHN F. KENNEDY

*There are no elements so diverse that they cannot
be joined in the heart of a man.*

—JEAN GIRAUDOUX

For Couples from Different Generations

If yours is an intergenerational marriage—congratulations!
The marriage of innocence and experience can make for
the perfect union.

Falling in love is always a cause for celebration because
it reminds us of being young, a time when anything was
possible. As we get older, we sometimes catch our own
image in the mirror, surprised by what we see because the
child in us doesn't know how old we are. Remember the
lesson of Scripture that "love never fails." When you are
saying your vows, perhaps make your vows a toast to love
. . . as long as you're both old enough to drink!

Age differences remind us that marriages aren't made because people look alike or think the same way. They happen because we complement each other. The highest compliment you can pay to your love is to be the best complement to your future spouse, by offering balance as he or she helps you find yours. During your vows don't shy away from acknowledging your differences or fail to point out your similarities. This is the perfect time to highlight all that makes you work so well together as a couple.

If you are of different ages, perhaps asking these questions of yourself and each other will assist you in the preparation of your vows:

- *How does your partner remind you that it's you that matters and not how old you are?*
- *What have you learned from each other that has nothing to do with how old you are?*
- *Write down five words that best describe your partner.*
- *Write down five words that you feel your partner would use to describe you.*
- *What activities do you like to do together?*
- *What do you like to do separately?*
- *What is the one trait of your partner's that you would most like to have?*

Quotations for Those of Different Generations

The longer I live the more beautiful life becomes.

—FRANK LLOYD WRIGHT

Though it sounds absurd, it is true to say I felt younger at sixty than I felt at twenty.

—ELLEN GLASGOW

It is a mistake to regard age as a downhill grade toward dissolution. The reverse is true. As one grows older, one climbs with surprising strides.

—GEORGE SAND

You're never too old to become younger.

—MAE WEST

The old shall dream dreams and the young shall see visions.

—JOEL 2:28

You don't stop laughing because you grow old. You grow old because you stop laughing.

—MICHAEL PRITCHARD

I am not young enough to know everything.

—OSCAR WILDE

When you have loved as she has loved, you grow old beautifully.

—W. SOMERSET MAUGHAM

Experience is what we call our mistakes.

—YIDDISH FOLK SAYING

Time and chance happen to all of us.

—ECCLESIASTES 9:11

To be old is a glorious thing when one has not unlearned what it means to begin.

—MARTIN BUBER

For Those Who Have Been Down the Aisle Before

If either of you or both have been down the aisle before, but you've found love again in each other—congratulations! At the root of all love is faith—faith in tomorrow, and faith that the future is not written in the past.

Too many people challenge others by accusing them of not being the person they once were. Actually, in life the challenge for all of us is to dare to be the person we might yet become. We are not here to meet anyone else's expectations. Life is a surprise, and we can expect to be surprised. Some of us who never felt we would fall in love again are nonetheless surprised to find that we have. And those of us who have had love snatched away by accident or illness know both the loss of what we are missing and love's capacity to fill that void.

Any of us remarrying need to remember that finding someone right doesn't mean we were wrong before. And choosing to believe in love might be the most "right" decision any of us can make. Certainly one has to question the wisdom of those who think otherwise.

Consider yourself truly blessed if you have the good fortune to find yourself in love and willing to commit yourself to another now that you're older and wiser, though still young at heart. Incorporate lessons you've learned in life into your vows, and mention significant (shared or otherwise) life events that hold meaning for both of you. If you have children in your lives, consider how you can involve them in the ceremony. The most exclusive weddings are often the most inclusive.

As you who have been down the aisle before now think about the vows you want to say to each other, perhaps asking these questions of yourself and each other will lend strength to your love:

- *What do you know about yourself now that you didn't know when you were younger?*
- *What is there in your heart that you have never given away until now?*
- *What have you learned about the nature of commitment?*
- *How will you guard each other's solitude?*
- *How would you like to look back on this relationship ten, twenty, or thirty years down the road?*
- *What is something wonderful that someone in your family or a friend has told you about your future spouse?*
- *How did you meet, and what was your mental state at the time you met?*
- *If you have children, what is something kind that one of them has said about your future spouse?*

• *How does your spouse feel about your children, and what role will he or she have in your children's lives?*

Consider the following examples of vows created by a couple, Michelle and Jim, experiencing a second wedding:

MICHELLE: *Jim, I never thought I would have the blessing of finding a man again that I would want to spend the rest of my life with, but you came into my life with your love for life and your passion for joy and turned my heart into a believer . . .*

JIM: *Michelle, my love and partner. You came into my life and I find myself laughing and smiling just being in your presence. Every day for the rest of our lives I promise to be true and respectful. Thank you for the opportunity to love again . . .*

Quotations for Those Who Have Been Married Before

The great man is he who does not lose his child's heart.

—MENCIUS

*Only when you have crossed the river can you say
the crocodile has a lump on its snout.*

—ASHANTI PROVERB

You cannot create experience. You must undergo it.

—ALBERT CAMUS

*Life is a series of lessons that must be lived to be
understood.*

—RALPH WALDO EMERSON

*It's choice—not chance—that determines your
destiny.*

—JEAN NIDETCH

*He who knows others is wise.
He who knows himself is enlightened.*

—LAO-TSU

*Don't walk behind me, I may not lead. Don't walk
in front of me, I may not follow. Just walk beside
me and be my friend.*

—ALBERT CAMUS

We arrive at various states of life quite as novices.

—LA ROCHEFOUCAULD

Experience is not what happens to you; it is what you do with what has happened to you.

—ALDOUS HUXLEY

Sample Vows Written by People Like You

What follows are some examples of personalized vows written by people just like you. The inclusion of these vows in this chapter is to help you remember that you don't have to choose between traditional vows and personalized vows, you can mix and match.

While some of what you read below may not sound like it was written by a professional poet or speechwriter, sounding professional is less important than being authentic. Let your vows ring with authenticity. For some of us little will resonate like the traditional, while for others traditional vows are only a starting point to creating something more personal.

I will forever love you and share with you my most intimate thoughts. I promise to love, hold, cherish, and value you above all else and above all others. I pledge to see things through your eyes, and to see you through thick and thin. I promise that as we grow old I will never forget what we have now and forever. No matter how many days pass, I know our love will not pass and will grow. These are my words from my heart to you—take them to your heart.

I offer you my love in every season of every year. I promise to always respect you and hope to always be worthy of your friendship and love. I pledge you will have my love and compassion in all that comes our way for better or for worse, in sickness and health, forever—if you will forever be mine. I give you all my intent to be the person closest to you and my complete intent to share the laughter and joy in life and bring more laughter and joy into your life. I treasure the memories of our individual pasts and look to the memories of our shared future.

This is my pledge to the woman I love, to the woman in my life who has been heaven sent. I promise to hug and kiss you every day—from now until eternity. I make this pledge with my whole heart.

I accept you and take you as my husband because you are also my friend, my loyal and respectful partner, my one true love. On this most special day, I give to you this most special promise. And I give it to you in the presence of all those I love and in the presence of those who also love you. I will be your wife. I will stand by your side. No one will divide us. No event will divide us. And time will not divide us, not in this life or the next. You are my lover; you are my friend.

I promise that when you are sad or scared or worried or confused, I will be there, right next to you. I pledge to be your wife through the good and bad, the better and best of life. I pledge, standing next to you on this day, to be your partner in life and in everything life brings us.

Our love started with a crazy adventure and then turned into the journey of our lives. How lucky I am to be standing here with you. I thank God for blessing us with each other. There is nothing more

I could ask than to have your company on the path ahead and in the years in front of us. I promise to pack love, happiness, and excitement into our backpacks and take you to be my husband on this journey through time.

I have been married before, but I have never been so much in love. I have promised to love before, but I have never understood what it meant to make that promise until you. I have felt alone before, but I have never felt alone since I met you. I have wondered what it would be like to grow old before, but now I thank God that I will grow old with you. I ask only one thing of you, will you marry me? You and I come from very different backgrounds and yet we come from one place because we come from love and have arrived at love together.

You and I never thought we would find each other, and now we can't imagine not having each other in our lives.

You and I are about to become one, and I promise you I will never undo what we are making because you have made me so happy. You are the one.

Additional Resources

The following are resources you can draw on to aid in your efforts to craft your vows or otherwise incorporate words of love into your ceremony. These are the assembled lyrical voices of poets and storytellers with ideas that sing to the heart. Perhaps you will hear one or more singing to you.

Love Poems from God: Twelve Sacred Voices from the East and West, Daniel James Ladinsky, ed., Penguin, 2002.

One Hundred and One Classic Love Poems, Contemporary Books, 1988.

Wedding Blessings: Prayers and Poems Celebrating Love, Marriage, and Anniversaries, June Cotner, ed., Broadway Books, 2003.

Wedding Readings: Centuries of Writing and Rituals on Love and Marriage, Eleanor C. Munro, ed., Penguin, 1996.

Love Poems, Everyman's Library, Sheila Kohler and Kevin Young, eds., Knopf, 1993.

Love Letters, Everyman's Library, Peter Washington and Kevin Young, eds., Knopf, 1996.

Marriage Poems, Everyman's Library, John Hollander and Kevin Young, eds., Knopf, 1997.

The Sonnets: Poems of Love, William Shakespeare, edited by William Burto, St. Martin's Press, 1980.

2

A World of Wedding Ceremonies

Don't marry someone you can live with; marry someone you can't live without.

—JOSH MCDOWELL

Tradition often plays a larger part in our lives than we realize. In a rapidly changing world, simply the urge for the familiar can cause tradition to tug at us during defining life moments. Your wedding is a perfect time to explore your background and that of your partner as well as the customs of others to determine what fits best for you and your loved one. This is the perfect opportunity to consider which aspects of these traditions you might want to incorporate into your ceremony.

Following are some cultural and religious customs from around the world and across time, reflecting the long history of wedding tradition. We take you through a broad but by no means encyclopedic compilation of humankind's expressions of love and commitment. Our aim has been, even in our brevity, to honor a variety of backgrounds. If your tradition is not included, please know this reflects no intentional disregard but only the dictates of space.

Our aim is to illustrate how lovers have joined their hearts in marriage through the ages. Drink from the wells of time and let your love find refreshment and nourishment.

Marriage in Roman Society

Marriage in Roman society was for the purpose of forming a family, to create lawful children. The word *matrimonium* is a derivative from *mater*, which means "mother." Marrying and having children would strengthen the honor of the family and escalate its ability to contribute to the state, so marrying was a way of showing that you were stable and had influence in the society. Furthermore, the emperor Augustus set penalties for men who were single for long periods of time.

The Romans as a social order gave a great deal of power to the father, and he was the one who arranged his children's marriages. This power, however, was not without checks and balances, as the son or daughter had to consent to the marriage before it was deemed legal. Before the father could agree to an arranged marriage, he would have to make sure that the couple was not related or in a relationship with another. Also they needed to have the legal right to marry. Slaves did not have that right, and many restrictions were placed on marriage for noncitizens and freed slaves. Soldiers on active duty also could not marry as they had to be free to fight for their society, although many married at the end of their military service.

Class was not the only determining factor in a father's decision to choose a bride for his son. A Roman man also considered the amount of money the bride's family had because it was the custom that they would pay for the wedding. If the bride's family was wealthy it would be looked upon as a good strategic decision for the man to start his political career, as men often did in their twenties, and a marriage was a way to create an economic and political partnership between two families.

Anglo-Saxon Wedding History

Most of the earlier weddings in Wales and England consisted of a simple informal ceremony with only the families present, during which the couple would make their vows of commitment to each other. The vows and the following sexual relationship would make the marriage legitimate. People did not conduct their vows in a church until the 1500s, and at that point it was still not mandatory.

Formal state involvement in marriages didn't begin until 1653, when the Civil Marriage Act, passed by the Puritans under Cromwell, required a civil ceremony before a justice of the peace. Prior to that, the bride's father would lead a public ceremony called a *bewedding*. During this ceremony, the groom and his family would pledge to the bride's parents that she would be well looked after.

It was not until 1753, with the introduction of Lord Hardwicke's Marriage Act, that all weddings had to take place in the Jewish synagogue, Church of England, or a Quaker meeting to be considered valid. Although this was the case, many resisted the government and church's involvement in their ceremony and chose to elope.

Chinese Wedding Traditions

In the Chinese tradition, before a wedding took place the two sets of parents exchanged the family credentials as a sign of intent for their children to marry. An exchange of gifts between the bride's and groom's families followed and represented several things: (1) that the groom's family acknowledged the parents' efforts in raising the bride and (2) the agreement that the groom has now formally been pledged the bride's hand in marriage by her parents. The exchange of gifts would continue for a year or two until the children were old enough to marry.

The groom's family would present a plethora of gifts to the bride's family, ranging from money to tea, bridal cakes, sweetmeats, and wine. The bride's family would in turn give gifts of food and clothing to the groom's family.

The bridal cakes that the bride's family received would be given to the groom's family and friends as a way to invite them to the wedding. The order in which the cakes were given out would be an indication of the recipients' seniority and degree of intimacy to the couple. Anyone who received a bridal cake was in turn expected to give a wedding gift as a token of congratulations to the bride's parents.

During a traditional Chinese ceremony, the bride and groom are taken to the family altar, where they pay respects to the Heaven and Earth, their family ancestors, and the Kitchen God. Tea is offered to the groom's parents, usually with two lotus seeds or two red dates in the cup. The lotus seeds and two red dates are used in the tea because the words *lotus* and *year*, *seed* and *child*, and *date* and *early* are homophones (they have the same sound in Chinese). The ancient Chinese believed that putting these items in the tea would help the newlyweds produce children early in their marriage and every year, which would ensure many grandchildren for the couple's parents. Also, the sweetness of the special tea is a wish for sweet relations between the bride and her new family.

To complete the marriage ceremony, the bride and groom bow to each other and drink wine from the same goblet. They might also eat sugar molded into the form of a rooster, which in Chinese astrology implies trustworthiness, a quality that certainly is central to a happy marriage. The ceremony tends to end with the bride and groom and their families participating in a wedding dinner together.

The Chinese present the couple with lucky money in red envelopes. Red and gold are colors of happiness and wealth. Wedding invitations, decorations, and gifts are all wrapped in red. Firecrackers are set off to frighten off evil spirits.

Japanese Wedding Traditions

During the traditional Japanese wedding ceremony, a tea ceremony takes place honoring and thanking the parents.

Drinks of sake (a rice wine) are exchanged between close family and friends to indicate their new unification.

Red and white are considered a happy color combination, and as such are used lavishly in the wedding ceremony. From the soup to the ice cream, even the foods at this festive occasion incorporate the joyful color scheme.

Modern Japanese weddings are celebrated in many different ways, including mixing traditional Japanese elements with Western wedding customs. Traditional Japanese wedding ceremonies are held in Shinto style at a shrine with the bride and groom both wearing kimonos. Shinto, the predominant religion in Japan, means "the way of the Kami." Kami are spiritual entities that can have great influence on human life. While it is a religion, in many ways it is also a collection of perspectives and thoughts thoroughly integrated into the Japanese aesthetic. Central to the Shinto religion is a harmony with the spirits.

After a series of symbolic rituals including waving the *haraiguishi*, the purification wand, the celebrant may open the service with the following ancient ritual prayer:

O Most High Ruler of Heaven,
O sun and moon and stars,
O King of the East on the left,

And Queen of the West on the right,
O five monarchs of the five directions,
O four seasons and four weathers:
We give to you a man and woman of happiness
And ask you to remove all great problems.
Give them abundance,
And allow them peace.

The sacred sake ceremony, *san-san-kudo,* holds a central place in the marriage ceremony. During this ceremony, nothing is said and the sacred silence speaks volumes.

Then follows a series of ritual offerings, at the conclusion of which the celebrant will clap twice and the bride and groom bow to each other. Following this, here is another example of the kind of sacred verse the celebrant may say as a way of spiritually focusing on the moment:

We pray You will receive in peace these offerings
of peace and plenty and sanctify the home of the
bride and groom forever, grant them abundance
and may their spirits live in peace in their home.

Unlike Western rituals, the bride and groom in a Shinto marriage do not tend to kiss after the vows. Here again, however, is another example of what traditionally might be said by the celebrant:

Bless this couple as you are stationary and forever.

May they live their lives flourishing and in good fortune like great trees.

May they as bride and groom, along with heaven and earth, sun and moon, offer light and radiance to us all.

Today, if a shrine isn't located nearby, the bride and groom might choose to have their wedding in the hotel where the reception takes place. A Shinto priest conducts the ceremony, which is witnessed by the very close family members. During the ceremony the couple is purified by drinking sake, and then the groom reads the words of commitment to the marriage. To close the ceremony, symbolic offerings of small tree twigs called *sakaki* are given to the Kami. The sakaki tree is a very auspicious tree in Japan, said to have holy powers and therefore be a favored home for Kami.

Korean Wedding Traditions

We lack space here to give a complete overview of a Korean ceremony, but the following are some interesting customs you may see if you participate in or attend a Korean wedding.

In some Korean weddings, the bride must take part in the traditional introduction ceremony where she is accepted into the groom's family before she can be married. After the newlyweds exchange vows the groom formally introduces his new bride to his parents.

Often, the Korean bride and groom share a special white wine, *jung jong*, with two cups formed from the two halves of a gourd. The bride and groom each take a sip from their cup, and then the two cups are mixed together and the couple drinks again signifying their new life together.

For good luck in fertility, the Korean groom's father might throw red dates at his new daughter-in-law.

Also, ducks and geese mate for life and represent faithfulness and many times are incorporated in a Korean wedding for their symbolism. There was a time when, if a man wanted to get married in Korea, he would arrive at his future bride's home on a white pony and present her family with a pair of geese.

Vietnamese Wedding Traditions

Because most Vietnamese are Mahayana Buddhists, the wedding dates are set by an astrologer. The first of the two separate wedding ceremonies takes place at the bride's home, the second at the groom's. When the groom and his family travel to the bride's house they carry painted trunks that are lined with pink satin (pink symbolizes happiness) and filled with many gifts of money, jewelry, and clothes. The groom's mother does not go along with her son, so that she does not appear to be a threat to or in competition with his new bride. Instead, on the morning of the wedding she brings pink chalk, symbolizing a rosy future, and betel nuts to sweeten the breath and aid in digestion of food. Also, the eating of betel leaves gives a sense of exhilaration and promotes positive cohabitation.

To enter the bride's home, the groom offers an entrance fee given in a red envelope and puts the gifts in front of the bride's ancestors' altar. The bride and groom then kneel in front of the altar while the bride's parents present the couple to her ancestors for their approval. Once this is done, the guests go to the groom's home. The guests of the wedding are served tea while the couple performs the altar ceremony once again, this time for the groom's ancestors.

After these ceremonies, cooked rice, which has been stained red to symbolize the wish for a prosperous life, is placed on the wedding altar. A boiled chicken and incense are laid before a separate wedding altar facing south. The chicken and the rising smoke from the incense represent the legend of the Phoenix and that the couple's love will never be consumed even as they grow old. The wedding altar faces south to avoid the extremes of hot and cold weather so that the couple's home life together will similarly avoid the extremes of temperament.

The groom's parents bow and invite the person marrying the couple to step forward and to ask the gods of marriage to bless the bride and groom. The officiant then binds the bride and groom together with a red thread and wraps the red thread around the altar. Now the couple is deemed married and the celebration begins with eating chicken and rice.

African Wedding Traditions

Africa is rich in cultural traditions, especially wedding and marriage rituals. The people of Africa celebrate the bonding of a woman and a man in a variety of ways, from being courted by cousins to kidnapping the bride-to-be. An important feature of African wedding tradition is that family has to be involved in the wedding for the marriage to be considered legitimate.

The African bride often wears a veil of braided hair as a symbol of modesty. Wine may be poured on the ground as an offering or libation to the gods. In Kenya, the bride

and groom are literally bound together during the ceremony with a leather band. Other regions in Africa also use
braided grasses for this tradition.

Marriages are arranged in the Swahili tribe of Kenya.
Before the ceremony, a number of rituals intended to
enhance the bride's attraction are performed. She is bathed
in oils and sandalwood and has henna designs temporar-
ily tattooed on her limbs. A *somo*, an elder woman of the
tribe, instructs the bride how to please her husband, and
may even hide under the bed in case there is a problem
consummating the marriage.

Among the Himba of Kenya, the groom and members
of his family kidnap the bride before the ceremony and
decorate her in an *ekori*, a marriage headdress made of
leather. When the bride arrives at her new husband's
home, his relatives tell her what her responsibilities as his
wife will be, and they show her their acceptance into their
family by anointing her with butterfat.

Weddings of the Ndebele of South Africa are celebrated in three stages, the end of which can take several
years. The first stage is negotiation of the wedding payment, or *lobola*, for the bride, which is paid in installments
of money and livestock. A two-week sequestration of the
bride is the second stage, during which time other women
teach the bride how to be a good wife. The third stage is
completed only when the bride has her first child.

In Ethiopian culture it is the woman who initiates the engagement. The bride proposes to the groom, and the groom then sends a cow to the bride's home so that her mother can make dairy products that in turn will be sent back to the groom as a gift. Once the bride proposes to the groom, the groom immediately starts helping the bride's father in the farm as well as her other relatives to prove his desire to be a real son.

During the wedding, a traditional wedding song is often used in tribes from southwestern Ethiopia. Dancers and singers form a circle around the bride. Then, using sticks, bells, drums, flutes, and horns, the festivities begin. At the end of the wedding ceremony the bride is escorted by a long line of her guests as they lead her to her new husband's house.

The African-American bride and groom during the days of slavery were not allowed to marry and so reached back into a long tradition from Africa called "jumping the broom." This simple ritual involved the eldest in the community placing a broom across the threshold and having the couple jump over the broom into their new home, symbolizing a crossing over into a new time in their lives. These days, the brooms can range from a collection of twigs and rags to bound cowrie shells and ribbons, beautifully decorated. Some of the brooms are kept as works of art in the couple's new home together. During the marriage ceremony the broom can be placed behind or in front of the altar or can be held up by a church elder or the celebrant.

It is believed that the broom held a spiritual significance, symbolizing the start of homemaking for the bride and groom. For the Kgatla people of southern Africa, tradition dictates that the day after the bride is married, she must use the broom to help the other women in the family sweep. They sweep the courtyard clean, and this represents her eagerness and duty to help with the housework at her new husband's parents' home until the newlyweds move into a home of their own.

The traditional African wedding clothing is a beautiful and colorful kente cloth. These days, many tuxedo retailers and formal suit rentals provide such pieces as a vest with this print. To symbolize fertility, cowrie shells are worn in bridal necklaces and also used to trim gowns and headpieces.

Hispanic Wedding Traditions

The customs and traditions tend to vary with each Latin-American country, and it would be unfair to try and sum them all up here in such a brief presentation. In addition, each Latin-American culture has been influenced both by the native cultures and the church. The following are a few of the varied traditions within the Latin-American community.

The Mexican groom gives a small chest of thirteen gold coins (for the twelve apostles and Jesus) to the bride, symbolizing giving wealth and strength, as a sign of his commitment to her. Near the end of the wedding the groom will pour the coins into the hands of the bride, now symbolizing that he is giving her control of his worldly goods. In some Mexican wedding ceremonies the couple is united symbolically with a *lazo*, or lasso. In this tradition a white rope braided into a figure eight (classically representing infinity and that the relationship should last forever) or a long rosary is draped around the pair.

In Venezuela, similar to Mexico, thirteen coins are often exchanged (although gold foiled chocolate coins are many times used as facsimiles). Here too the coins are a symbol of future good fortune and prosperity.

In some Latin-American countries there are wedding sponsors called *padrinos* and *madrinas* who promise financial and spiritual aid. There may be separate sponsors for flowers, the *lazo* ceremony, or even furniture or appliances for the new couple's home.

In Puerto Rico, a bridal doll in a dress that is a duplicate of the gown of the bride is put at the head of the cake table. On the doll's dress little mementos called *capias* are pinned. As the bride and groom walk around to greet the guests and thank them for attending the wedding, they pin each guest with a *capia*.

In Peru it is a custom to include wedding charms between the layers of the wedding cake, attached with ribbons. Before the cake is cut and served to the guests, any woman who is not married pulls a string. The unmarried woman who pulls the ribbon with the "ring" on the end is to marry within a year.

Spanish Traditions

In traditional Spanish weddings the groom is dressed in a tucked shirt that is hand embroidered by the bride. The bride carries orange blossoms in her bouquet, which add a beautiful scent to the festivities.

Before the wedding ceremony, the groom gives the bride thirteen coins, an act that is called the giving of *monedas* or *arras*. These coins represent the groom's ability to support and take care of the bride. During the wedding ceremony the bride will carry the coins in a special purse, or else a young girl will carry them on a pillow or a handkerchief.

Indian Traditions

Indian marriages across the subcontinent reflect similar basic religious rites but with regional colors and customs overlaying depending on where the bride and groom live. Many of the rituals and traditions that were started in the Vedic times, a time of Indo-Aryan invasion and rule from 1500 B.C., are still followed in Hindu marriages. For example, a Hindu marriage usually begins with a *muhurat*, or favorable time, astrologically, of the year on a day when the "bright half" of the northern course of the sun is occurring, which makes good luck more auspicious and bad luck less likely. The wedding ceremony and reception most often take place at the bride's family's home.

In the *Mehendi* ceremony, a spiritual ceremony that "kicks off" the wedding ceremony, henna paste is applied as a token to the groom's hands while the bride's hands and feet are painted with intricate patterns. These varied patterns signify the strength of love in marriage. The darker the color, the stronger the love and bond will be.

An awning called a *mandapa* is decorated with flowers, creating a stage for the wedding. Turmeric is rubbed on the bride and groom to serve as a ritualistic healing and cleansing.

The main event for the groom is the *baraat*, the groom's wedding procession, an event that starts with a glorious display of fireworks and the enthusiastic dancing of family and friends to music. This is a time for both sides of the family to greet the groom and share in his joy. When the groom arrives, the bride's mother welcomes him with a garland of flowers and leads him to the *mandapa*.

The *mangalsutra*, a necklace generally made out of two strings of small black beads with a gold pendant, is tied by the groom around his bride's neck. The black beads are believed to act as protection against evil. Married women wear this to protect their marriage and the life of their husband. It is the Indian equivalent of the Western wedding ring. In southern India, the mangalsutra is called *tali*, and is a small gold ornament strung on a cotton cord or a gold chain.

Punjabi (Sikh) Marriage Traditions

Punjab is a state in the north of India, home to many who practice the Sikh religion. A Sikh marriage is very much like the Hindu marriage ceremony. One important difference, however, is that the religious texts that the Sikhs use are not Vedic texts, but from the *Guru Granth Sahib*, the supreme spiritual text of the Sikh religion.

A Sikh wedding is described as *Anand Karaj*—a ceremony of bliss. Before the wedding, a three-day wedding path is held and is considered to be one of the main ceremonies. The wedding shopping begins by purchasing a *Rumalla*. This is a set of four pieces of cloth used to cover the *Granth Sahib*. This is often an expensive fabric, which is intricately embroidered. Only after this purchase is the rest of the shopping done.

As part of the engagement, the bride's family goes to the groom's house with all kinds of sweets, fruits, and dry fruits and other gifts of clothes and jewelry. A part of the dowry, if there is one, is also carried on this occasion. The bride's father (or in his absence the brother or any other older male member of the family) gives the would-be groom a gold ring, a *kara* (bangle), with a minimum of eleven gold *mohra* (sovereigns). These are later strung onto a black thread and put around the girl's neck after the wedding. It's like the mangalsutra that the Hindus wear, but is not worn by the bride around the neck thereafter. She normally wears it only on occasions such as family weddings.

The groom's family, usually close female relatives, comes to the bride's house with the wedding veil, which is made of traditionally embroidered chiffon or chignon fabric. The bride is also given a ring and other jewelry as well as clothes. The groom's mother puts a bit of *mehendi* (henna) on the bride's palms in intricate patterns to declare her engaged. The ladies' music begins to the beat of the *dholki* (drums) and signals the beginning of the bride's confinement to the house till her marriage. Traditionally, the marriage ceremony is an affair spread over at least ten days. The families believed in guarding the girl against any mishap in this period. These days, however, the confinement is only for a day.

In Punjabi tradition, the bride's maternal uncle plays a very important role in the *Chuda* ceremony preparing the bride for the wedding. Her family members on her mother's side give her the wedding dress, which is usually made with bright colors such as orange, red, and a bright pink. The groom usually dresses up in a formal suit or a light-color safari suit.

On the day of the wedding ceremony, there is a formal introduction of the close relatives of the bride and groom to each other. During the wedding ceremony, the bride's father puts a ring on the groom's finger; this represents that his daughter is now in the care of her husband. At the end of the ceremony the bride's uncle ties dangling metal plates to the bride. The custom is that just when the bride is going to say goodbye to everyone at the end of the celebration, she hits one of her cousins or friends with these plates and this person is the lucky one to next be married.

Pakistani (Muslim) Wedding Traditions

Pakistan is a country that subscribes to Muslim traditions. In Muslim society, a marriage is a contract between two parties, a man and a woman. The contract is made in the presence of witnesses as well as the woman's guardian. It also involves the payment of a dowry to her family, the amount of which is agreed between the two parties.

The offer of marriage is made by the woman's father or guardian, and the acceptance must be made by the groom in the presence of two Muslim witnesses. The witnesses may be required to testify to the marriage in front of a judge. (Witness testimony is binding on a Muslim party only if all parties are Muslim.)

Note that while there are many countries with Muslim majority populations and Muslim legal traditions, each of these countries also has cultural traditions that are often integrated into the wedding. As one might suspect, long-term geographic proximity of Pakistan to India is reflected in varying aspects of Indian (rather than Hindu) traditions often finding their way into Pakistani wedding ceremonies.

In Pakistan, the wedding celebration lasts anywhere from seven to ten days. During this time, the men and women are not allowed to interact freely. The actual contract of the marriage happens at the groom's house. The gifts tend to be jewelry in gold.

One of the very special things about a Pakistani wedding is the amount of festivity, a reminder that a wedding ceremony, while sacred, is also fun. A Pakistani wedding has three parts: *mehndi*, *shadi*, and *valima*.

Mehndi, the first part, is a ceremony that takes place before the wedding. It may occur on the night before the wedding, or it can last up to two days. During this time, henna is painted onto the couple's hands in beautiful and intricate patterns. The ceremony itself is full of traditional dances and songs.

Shadi is the second part of the wedding. Hosted by the bride's parents, it is when the marriage paperwork is officially signed. This is called the *Nikah*. This process takes place in the attendance of an imam, an Islamic prayer leader. The bride is dressed in an elaborately embroidered outfit with all of the best jewelry, but she does not come out to join the others until after the signing. The rest of the guests, especially the women, wear brightly colored dresses and jewelry.

The third and last part of the Pakistani wedding is called the *valima*. This is a reception that is held on the day after the wedding and is hosted by the groom's parents.

Jewish Wedding Traditions

A traditional Jewish wedding is full of meaningful rituals, giving expression to the deepest significance and purpose of marriage. In fact, the traditional wedding custom of the bride wearing "something blue" with her wedding dress originated in ancient Israel. An Israeli bride wore a blue ribbon, symbolizing fidelity.

The wedding day heralds the happiest and holiest day of one's life, for on this day all the bride's and groom's past mistakes are forgiven as they merge into a new, complete soul. As on Yom Kippur, the couple fast from dawn until after the completion of the marriage ceremony, and in a very traditional ceremony the groom wears a *kittel*, the traditional white robe worn on Yom Kippur.

It is customary among some for the bride and groom not to see each other during the week preceding the wedding. Separate receptions, called *Kabbalat Panim*, are held just prior to the wedding ceremony. Next comes the *badeken*, the veiling of the bride by the groom. The veil symbolizes modesty and conveys the lesson that however attractive physical appearances may be, the soul and character are paramount.

The wedding ceremony takes place under a canopy called the *chupah*, a symbol of the home to be built and shared by the couple. It is open on all sides as a symbol of welcome and unconditional hospitality to friends and relatives.

Under the *chupah*, the groom circles the bride seven times. Just as the world was created in seven days, the groom is figuratively building the walls of the couple's new home. The number seven also symbolizes the wholeness and completeness that they can attain separately. Another explanation is that seven circles corresponds to the seven times in the Torah where it is written ". . . and when a man takes a wife."

The wedding ring is traditionally made of plain gold, without ornamentation (such as stones) — just as it is hoped that the marriage will be one of simple beauty.

The ceremony contains a reading of the *ketubah* (marriage contract) in the original Aramaic text. In marriage, the groom accepts certain marital responsibilities, which are detailed in the *ketubah*; his principal obligations are to provide food, shelter, and clothing for his wife, and to be attentive to her emotional needs.

Near the end of the ceremony, a glass is placed on the floor and the groom shatters it with his foot. This act serves as an expression of sadness at the destruction of the Temple in Jerusalem, and identifies the couple with the spiritual and national destiny of the Jewish people. (Some explain that this is the last time the groom gets to "put his foot down"!) This marks the conclusion of the ceremony, and the couple are escorted to a private room and left alone for the first time. This time of seclusion is called the *yichud*, and it affords the couple a few moments together before joining their guests. When the couple has fasted until the ceremony, this is their opportunity to break the fast with either a chicken soup or their favorite food. These moments of seclusion signify the newly acquired right of the bride and groom to live together as husband and wife.

Roman Catholic Traditions

The traditional Roman Catholic wedding takes place in the sacrament of matrimony. A Catholic ceremony will include several relevant biblical readings, the exchange of vows and rings, the Prayer of the Faithful, the nuptial blessing, prayers, and music.

The Roman Catholic wedding is full of tradition and literature. The wedding ceremony is a time to worship as well as to join the couple in matrimony.

While some marriage ceremonies are private, the Roman Catholic traditional ceremony is usually quite a public custom. To begin with, the marriage is celebrated in a community prayer space, usually the church building. The wedding guests are invited to the ceremony in order to witness the event and to participate in the liturgy.

The tradition of the sacrament more often than not happens during a nuptial Mass that takes place in the morning or in the early afternoon. The couple and the wedding party members are encouraged to receive the sacrament of reconciliation before receiving the sacrament of matrimony. Traditionally, the wedding takes place in the parish church of the bride's family.

Ancient Greek Weddings

In ancient Greek weddings the most lavish prewedding ceremony was the feast. The feast was held at the bride's father's home the day before the wedding took place. After the feast, the bride-to-be made sacrifices of childhood items such as dolls, toys, or clothing. This ritual represented that the bride was no longer a child. The wedding began with what was called "the giving of a pledge into the hand." This is a pact between the groom and the father of the bride. Below is an example:

FATHER OF THE BRIDE: *I give you this girl that she may bring children into the world within the bond of wedlock.*

GROOM: *I accept her.*

FATHER OF THE BRIDE: *I agree to provide a dowry of three talents (the largest standard silver piece in ancient Greece) with her.*

GROOM: *I accept that too—with pleasure.*

Even after this exchange of vows between the father of the bride and the groom, it was not until later on in the evening once she was home that the bride would unveil for her new groom.

Native American Traditions

At the center of Native American spirituality is the Great Spirit. This sacred force permeates all aspects of the universe. Similarly, it is the human responsibility within this spirituality to watch over and protect all forces of nature in the universe as each is a reflection of the Great Spirit.

Approximately two million Native Americans live in North America, and of this number about half consider themselves Christian. Native American wedding vows and traditions vary according to each tribe's geography, history, and language.

Because nature holds such a central place in Native American culture, getting married out of doors is common. Also, because the sun is seen as a manifestation of the Great Spirit, having the wedding party face east reflects connection and respect. Similarly, waving burning bundles of sage, or *smudging*, adds an atmosphere of purification at the beginning of the ceremony. The following is a traditional Native American affirmation of love in marriage:

> *My feet run because of you.*
> *My feet dance because of you.*
> *My heart beats because of you.*
> *My eyes see because of you.*
> *My mind thinks because of you.*
> *And I shall love because of you.*

Native American weddings have traditions as varied as the tribes themselves. The Pueblo bride and groom drink from a pottery vessel with two spouts. Drinking from this wedding vessel confirms the marriage.

The Hopi bride on the morning of her wedding has her hair washed with a soap made from yucca root as a means of purification. Later, small pieces of hair are cut from both the bride and groom and tied together. As in so many traditions, when the two strands are tied together, the couple is considered united. To the Hopi corn or maize was an essential food and represented fertility and the life force. Just before the wedding feast, the Hopi groom takes a handful of corn mush from the east side of a special wedding basket, the sacred direction where the sun rises, and feeds some to his bride before having some himself. After this, the bride will take corn from the west, north, south, and center of the basket for herself thereby centering her and her husband to the universe.

Cherokee weddings were unique to the community or clan, although almost all the varied communities used many of the same ritual elements. First and foremost, it was forbidden to marry within your clan.

In the Cherokee culture, women rather than men represent the family at the wedding ceremony. On a bride's wedding day she is given by her mother and oldest brother, and the groom is given by his mother.

During ancient times, the bride and groom would meet before the wedding party and exchange venison and an ear of corn. Venison symbolized the groom's intention to keep meat in the household, and the bride's ear of corn symbolized her willingness to care for and provide nourishment for her household.

During the wedding ceremony, songs are sung in the native Cherokee language to bless the couple. Then the bride and groom are first each covered in a blue blanket, then the blue blankets are shed and the couple is covered together by family members in a white blanket representing peace, fulfillment, and the beginning of their new life together.

In ancient Aztec wedding traditions the symbol of union was when the parents of the bride and groom would tie the capes of the two newlyweds together. During the Aztec vows, the bride and groom shared food and drink from five different clay vessels, the clay representing unity with the earth. They partook of water, signifying pure love; honey, for the sweet times the couple would share; lemon juice, for the bitter times in the relationship; coffee, signifying the dark times they would endure together; and a tamale, a symbol for the nourishment the couple would provide for each other.

Indonesian Traditions

In Indonesia, the groom employs a scholar, a man educated in religion, to initiate the marriage proposal with the bride's father. The groom goes with the scholar to the father's house, and the scholar speaks on behalf of the groom. The purpose of the scholar is to make the bride's family more open to the possibility of marriage.

The Indonesian bride and groom share rice seasoned with turmeric following the vows. Rice is a long-held symbol of fertility and prosperity, while the yellow turmeric is a reflection of everlasting love. As the couple share eating this rice three times, they are making the final vows binding them to one another.

As in many other traditions, the day of the wedding ceremony in Indonesian tradition is one of family and friends feasting and celebrating together. What is different is what happens after the wedding but is still considered part of the wedding ceremony.

After the wedding comes a testing period for the couple in which the groom and bride go to her family's house for four days and then move to his family's house for another four days. Once these back-and-forth four-day visits have ended, the family members of the groom and bride get together and decide what issues the new couple needs to work on for the honeymoon, which lasts for three months. During the honeymoon the bride and groom again stay at her family's home, and the groom's work is to spend this time trying to make his new bride happy. Once the three months are over—but only after the three months are over and the parental suggestions heeded—the couple's new married life together actually begins.

Snapshots of Traditions from Around the World

The following are a few snapshots of more ceremonial traditions from around the globe that you may want to incorporate in your wedding or may simply interest you.

The parents of the Turkish groom often bring a sweet desert that is distributed to the bride's family when the engagement is agreed upon, and during the wedding prayers a wedding flag is often planted by the groom's friends.

The Polynesian bride and groom arrive at the wedding ceremony in an outrigger canoe. The bride is then taken to a grass hut where she is massaged with a coconut oil infused with floral scents.

The Samoan bride wears a bridal dress woven from the bark of a mulberry tree, which according to tradition adds to her fertility.

The Scandinavian bride often wears an elaborate jeweled wedding dress as a symbol of innocence, while fiddlers and horns accompany the wedding procession to the church.

The Australian bride sometimes carries a horseshoe for good luck. The horseshoe is not an actual metal plate, but is crocheted, and a long ribbon is attached in a loop from end to end. The horseshoe is worn upside down over the arm of the bride during the wedding to bring luck to the marriage.

The Celtic tradition of tying a knot around the couple's hands is the source of the term "tying the knot." The roots of this go all the way back to medieval days, when knots were often used in images of weddings because they were said to represent hope, fidelity, and luck.

The Laotian bride and groom have their hands bound together with white cotton threads, which represent blessings and good luck.

In Wales, the bride wears a special pin on her bridal gown. After the ceremony, she must take it off and throw it over her shoulder for another to catch so that she will have a happy marriage.

The French throw laurel leaves (traditionally representing immortality since the original Olympic games and hence longevity in a marriage) outside the church as the couple depart.

The Irish couple is showered in flower petals for good luck, and the groom is held up in a chair to symbolize to all that he is now a married man. In Ireland, the bride's bouquet must contain English lavender or it is thought to be incomplete. The lavender adds fragrance and beauty to the bouquet, and also has a long tradition of bringing good luck and helping to ensure that the bride's wishes come true.

At a German wedding eve party, dishes are broken for good luck, borrowing from a tradition that the couple should have so much good luck and prosperity that a few broken dishes won't matter.

The Ukrainian wedding party has a similar tradition called *Vatana*. In this wedding custom, the dishes at the reception are broken with silver dollars—reflecting projected prosperity for the couple. In the Ukraine, couples also share *korovai* rather than a cake. *Korovai* is a sacred wedding bread decorated with symbolic images that represent eternity and the joining together of two families.

In Norway, *Brudlaupskling*, a wedding "cake" made of bread, dates back to the days when white flour was rare on Norwegian farms, and foods containing it were greatly admired. The bread is topped with a mixture of cheese, cream, and syrup, then folded over and cut into small squares.

Iranian couples share in a *Sofreh Aghed*, which dates back 2,500 years to Persia and literally means "the marriage spread." The couple and guests sit around this large spread of food while vows are said. At one point in the service, a sheer cloth is held over the heads of the couple while the bride's and groom's mothers rub two loaves of sugar together over them, implying that only sweetness and happiness shall rain on their children's marriage.

The Moroccan couple drinks sweetened milk and shares a date, signifying that they will share in the sweetness of life.

During a Jamaican wedding the bride's matron of honor is known as the Chief, and the flower girl carries the train. Curried goat and rice is included on the menu. Rum punch, including a red sweet fruit syrup, rum pimento, and lime is traditionally served. The wedding cake, usually a dark fruitcake, has been soaked in rum for about a year so the fruits and cake will be flavored and moist. The wedding reception often lasts until the sun comes up. With Jamaican hospitality, no guests are refused, even if they come uninvited.

Greeks give candy-coated almonds (almonds in biblical symbolism represent inner goodness and a good life) as favors to each of the wedding guests. Italian couples give bags of sugared almonds, symbolizing the bitterness and sweetness of life, to their guest to take home as memories.

We hope you have enjoyed this collection of wedding traditions from around the world. Remember, you don't have to be from one of these cultures to borrow from its wedding traditions to enrich your ceremony.

3

A World of
Wedding Vows

Love me tender, love me sweet, never let me go.
— ELVIS PRESLEY

All faiths have different branches of belief and orthodoxy, and this chapter aims to serve as a deep well of centuries-old learning and love you can draw on and drink from. While we have tried to gather wedding vows from a variety of different faiths and cultures, what follows is by no means an exhaustive compilation, but rather a sampling. Read these vows out loud and think about the meaning of each one. Are there words or phrases you might like to use to describe the commitment you and your partner are about to make?

You should check with your officiant and your own conscience before adopting any of these vows into your ceremony. If yours is a religious ceremony, you may not be able to customize the vows, but you can incorporate the messages contained in this chapter in other areas of your ceremony, including your program, speeches, and favors. Regardless of how you choose to use the information in this chapter, there is much to learn from the rituals of cultures and religions past and present and the value they place on love and fidelity in marriage. Do not hesitate to learn and borrow from the experiences of others—they can only enrich your own.

Issues of faith and religion are by their very definition personal matters. While all of us have a window in our soul that allows us to look out, we can't presume to look into the soul of another. As you prepare for your wedding, check in with your soul and your soul mate. Whatever tradition or religion you were raised in, are rebelling from, or are drawn to, use this chapter as a resource and a point of discussion to help you and your future husband or wife find a way to best describe your commitment to each other.

We live in an age of uncertainty. Love and marriage are statements of faith in the face of this uncertainty.

Roman Catholic Vows

I, (name), take you, (name), to be my (husband/
wife). I promise to be true to you in good times
and in bad, in sickness and in health. I will love
you and honor you all the days of my life.

BRIDE: I pledge, in honesty and sincerity, to be
for you an obedient and faithful wife.

GROOM: I pledge, in honesty and sincerity, to be
for you an obedient and faithful husband.

I, (name), take you, (name), for my wife/husband,
to have and to hold, from this day forward, for
better, for worse, for richer, for poorer, in sickness
and in health, until death do us part.

Lutheran Vows

I, (name), take you, (name), to be my (husband/
wife), and these things I promise you: I will be
faithful to you and honest with you; I will respect,
be truthful, help, and care for you; I will share my
life with you; I will forgive you as we have been

forgiven; and I will try with you to better
understand ourselves, the world, and God;
through the best and the worst of what is to come
as long as we live.

Methodist Vows

I, (name) ask you, (name), to be my husband/wife
as my friend and my love. On this day I affirm
the relationship we have enjoyed, looking to the
future to deepen and strengthen it. I will be yours
in plenty and in want, in sickness and in health,
in failure and in triumph. Together we will dream,
will stumble but restore each other, we will share
all things, serving each other and our fellow
humanity. I will cherish and respect you, comfort
and encourage you, be open with you, and stay
with you as long as we shall live, freed and bound
by our love.

Presbyterian Vows

I, (name), take thee, (name), to be my wedded
wife/husband, and I do promise and covenant,

before God and these witnesses, to be thy loving and faithful wife/husband; in plenty and in want, in joy and in sorrow, in sickness and in health, as long as we both shall live.

This ring I give you, in token and pledge of our constant faith and abiding love.

Episcopalian Vows

In the name of God, I, (name), take you, (name), to be my husband/wife, to have and to hold from this day forward, for better or worse, for richer or poorer, in sickness and health, to love and to cherish, until we are parted by death. This is my solemn vow.

Quaker Vows

In the presence of God and these, our Friends, I take thee to be my wife/husband, promising with Divine assistance to be unto thee a loving and faithful wife/husband as long as we both shall live.

The Quaker certificate of marriage:

On this the (day), (month), in the year of our Lord, (year), (both names) appeared together, and (groom's name) taking (bride's name) by the hand, did, on this solemn and joyous occasion, declare that he took (bride's name) to be his wife, promising with Divine assistance to be unto her a loving and faithful husband; and then, in the same assembly, (bride's name) did in like manner declare that she took (groom's name) to be her husband, promising with Divine assistance to be unto him a loving and faithful wife. And moreover they, (groom's name) and (bride's name), did, as further confirmation thereof, then and there, to this certificate set their hands.

And we, having been present at the marriage, have as witnesses hereunto set our hands.

Zion Vows

MINISTER: *(Groom), do you take (bride) to be your wedded wife, to live together after God's* *ordinance in holy matrimony? Do you promise to love her, to honor and cherish her, in joy and in sorrow, in sickness and in health, and to be to her in all things a good and faithful husband as long as you both shall live?*

GROOM: *I do.*

MINISTER: *(Bride), do you take (groom) to be your wedded husband, to live together after God's ordinance in holy matrimony? Do you promise to love him, to honor and cherish him, in joy and in sorrow, in sickness and in health, and to be to him in all things a good and faithful wife as long as you both shall live?*

BRIDE: *I do.*

MINISTER WITH GROOM REPEATING: *I, (name), take thee, (name), to be my wedded wife, to have and to hold, from this day forward, for better, for worse, for richer, for poorer, in sickness and in health, to love and to cherish, 'til death do us part. According to God's holy ordinance, and thereto I pledge thee my faith.*

MINISTER WITH BRIDE REPEATING: *I, (name), take thee, (name), to be my wedded husband, to*

*have and to hold, from this day forward, for
better, for worse, for richer, for poorer, in sickness
and in health, to love and to cherish, 'til death do
us part. According to God's holy ordinance, and
thereto I pledge thee my faith.*

GROOM: *I promise you, (name), that I will be
your loving and loyal husband from now on. I will
share with you all of life's joy and sorrow,
pleasure and pain, until death parts us.*

BRIDE: *I promise you, (name), that I will be your
loving and loyal wife from now on. I will share
with you all of life's joy and sorrow, pleasure and
pain, until death parts us.*

Jewish Vows

RABBI: *Do you, (groom), take (bride) to be your
wife?*

GROOM: *I do.*

RABBI: *Do you promise to love, cherish, and
protect her, whether in good fortune or in*

adversity, and to seek with her a life hallowed by the faith of Israel?

GROOM: *I do.*

RABBI: *Do you, (bride), take (groom) to be your husband?*

BRIDE: *I do.*

RABBI: *Do you promise to love, cherish, and protect him, whether in good fortune or in adversity, and to seek with him a life hallowed by the faith of Israel?*

BRIDE: *I do.*

RABBI: *(Groom), as you place this ring upon the finger of (bride), speak to her these vows: "With this ring be thou consecrated unto me as my wife, according to the law of God and the faith of Israel."*

(Bride), as you place this ring upon the finger of (groom), speak to him these vows: "With this ring be thou consecrated unto me as my husband, according to the law of God and the faith of Israel."

Celtic Vows

You cannot possess me for I belong to myself. But while we both wish it, I give you that which is mine to give.

You cannot command me, for I am a free person. But I shall serve you in those ways you require and the honeycomb will taste sweeter coming from my hand.

I pledge to you that yours will be the name I cry aloud in the night and the eyes into which I smile in the morning.

I pledge to you the first bite of my meat and the first drink from my cup.

I pledge to you my living and my dying, each equally in your care.

I shall be a shield for your back and you for mine.

I shall not slander you, nor you me.

I shall honor you above all others, and when we quarrel we shall do so in private and tell no strangers our grievances.

This is my wedding vow to you.

This is the marriage of equals.

Celtic Handfasting and Declaration of Intent

OFFICIANT: *(Groom), will you cause her pain?*

GROOM: *I may.*

OFFICIANT: *Is that your intent?*

GROOM: *No.*

OFFICIANT: *(Bride), will you cause him pain?*

BRIDE: *I may.*

OFFICIANT: *Is that your intent?*

BRIDE: *No.*

OFFICIANT: *(To both): Will you share each other's pain and seek to ease it?*

BRIDE AND GROOM: *Yes.*

OFFICIANT: *And so the binding is made. Join your hands.*

(The first cord is draped across the bride and groom's hands.)

OFFICIANT: *(Bride), will you share his laughter?*

BRIDE: *Yes.*

OFFICIANT: *(Groom), will you share her laughter?*

GROOM: *Yes.*

OFFICIANT: *(To both): Will both of you look for the brightness in life and the positive in each other?*

BRIDE AND GROOM: *Yes.*

OFFICIANT: *And so the binding is made.*

(The second chord is draped across the couple's hands.)

OFFICIANT: *(Bride), will you burden him?*

BRIDE: *I may.*

OFFICIANT: *Is that your intent?*

BRIDE: *No.*

OFFICIANT: *(Groom), will you burden her?*

GROOM: *I may.*

OFFICIANT: *Is that your intent?*

GROOM: *No.*

OFFICIANT: *(To both): Will you share the burdens of each so that your spirits may grow in this union?*

BRIDE AND GROOM: *Yes.*

OFFICIANT: *And so the binding is made.*

(The third cord is draped across the couple's hands.)

OFFICIANT: *(Bride), will you share his dreams?*

BRIDE: *Yes.*

OFFICIANT: *(Groom), will you share her dreams?*

GROOM: *Yes.*

OFFICIANT: *(To both): Will you dream together to create new realities and hopes?*

BRIDE AND GROOM: *Yes.*

OFFICIANT: *And so the binding is made.*

(The fourth cord is draped across the couple's hands.)

OFFICIANT: *(Groom), will you cause her anger?*

GROOM: *I may.*

OFFICIANT: *Is that your intent?*

GROOM: *No.*

OFFICIANT: *(Bride), will you cause him anger?*

BRIDE: *I may.*

OFFICIANT: *Is that your intent?*

BRIDE: *No.*

OFFICIANT: *(To both): Will you take the heat of anger and use it to temper the strength of this union?*

BRIDE AND GROOM: *We will.*

OFFICIANT: *And so the binding is made.*

(The fifth cord is draped across the couple's hands.)

OFFICIANT: *(Bride), will you honor him?*

BRIDE: *I will.*

OFFICIANT: *(Groom), will you honor her?*

GROOM: *I will.*

OFFICIANT: *(To both): Will you seek to never give cause to break that honor?*

BRIDE AND GROOM: *We shall never do so.*

Buddhist Vows

Because of the secularity of Buddhist weddings, there is no assigned set of marriage vows. However, the bride and groom will recite their expected undertakings using the *Sigilovdda Sutta* as a guide. The *Sigiloydda Sutta* says:

GROOM: *Toward my wife I undertake to love and respect her, be kind and considerate, be faithful, delegate domestic management, provide gifts to please her.*

BRIDE: *Toward my husband I undertake to perform my household duties efficiently, be hospitable to my in-laws and friends of my* *husband, be faithful, protect and invest our earnings, discharge my responsibilities lovingly and conscientiously.*

Hindu Vows

In Hinduism, each important occasion begins by inviting God into the ceremony. Here is a traditional example of this invocation:

You are unborn, total, and formless.

You are beyond bliss and yet are endless bliss.

You are free of attributes or any desires.

You are the Supreme Spirit and we pray to you.

The bride's sari is tied to the groom's scarf signifying an eternal bond that will keep them together. Then this prayer, or a similar one, is chanted in Sanskrit, the ancient language of India.

To you God, whom all prayers praise,

You have willed that this groom (name) and this bride (name) become husband and wife.

May you, the Divine Spirit, bear witness to this.

And now by their holding hands,

May they come to live as one in happiness and give birth to healthy, happy children.

May they always lend each other good company and across time become old together in a state of peace and happiness.

Perhaps the most important sacred rite in the marriage involves the bride and groom, hand in hand, taking seven steps around the sacred fire, *mangal fera*, where offerings have earlier been thrown by the bride's family. During this rite, the bride and groom make seven promises to each other. Here is an example of the seven traditional vows that are said during the "seven steps":

Let us take the first step to provide for our household a nourishing and pure diet, avoiding those foods injurious to healthy living. Let us take the second step to develop physical, mental, and spiritual powers. Let us take the third step to increase our wealth by righteous means and proper use. Let us take the fourth step to acquire knowledge, happiness, and harmony by mutual love and trust. Let us take the fifth step so that we be blessed with strong, virtuous, and heroic children. Let us take the sixth step for self-restraint and longevity. Finally, let us take the seventh step and be true companions and remain lifelong partners by this wedlock.

We have taken the Seven Steps. May the night be honey-sweet for us; may the morning be honey-sweet for us; may the earth be honey-sweet for us and the heavens be honey-sweet for us. May the plants be honey-sweet for us; may the sun be all honey for us; may the cows yield us honey-sweet milk. As the heavens are stable, as the earth is stable, as the mountains are stable, as the whole universe is stable, so may our union be permanently settled.

Baha'i Vows

In nineteenth-century Persia, what we now know as Iran, Baha'u'llah founded the Baha'i faith. The tenets of this religion say that God's universal message was conveyed through a series of messengers through the course of history including Abraham, Buddha, Jesus, Krishna, Moses,

Muhammad, Zoroaster, and Baha'u'llah. It is thought that all the messengers spoke the same language and urged humanity toward spiritual and moral considerations and to treat all others as equals. To Baha'u'llah, marriage is seen as "a fortress for well-being and salvation and that the partners should be loving companions for one another across time and eternity." Here are a few thoughts from Abdu'l Baha, (1844–1921), the eldest son of founding father Baha'u'llah, that you may want to draw on if you wish to incorporate Baha'i into your vows:

> *Love gives life to those without life. Love ignites a flame in the heart that is cold. Love brings hope to those without hope, and makes happy the heart of the saddened.*

> *These two souls are not only physical but also spiritual and heavenly and should be considered as one soul.*

> *In the world of humanity the greatest king is love. If love were extinguished . . . human life would disappear.*

> *Humanity has two wings—the male and female. If these two wings are not of equal strength, the bird will not fly.*

Civil Ceremony Vows

(Name), I take you to be my lawfully wedded (husband/wife). Before these witnesses I vow to love you and care for you as long as we both shall live.

I take you, with all your faults and strengths, as I offer myself to you with all my faults and strengths.

I will help you when you need help, and turn to you when I need help. I choose you as the person with whom I will spend my life.

I, (name), take you, (name), to be my wife/husband.

To share the good times and hard times side by side.

I humbly give you my hand and my heart as a sanctuary of warmth and peace, and pledge my faith and love to you.

Just as this circle is without end, my love for you is eternal.

Just as it is made of incorruptible substance, my commitment to you will never fail. With this ring, I thee wed.

Before our friends and those so special to us here, on this wonderful day of gladness and good fortune, I, (name), take you, (name), as my wife/husband, in friendship and in love, in strength and weakness, to share the good times and misfortune, in achievement and failure, to celebrate life with you forevermore.

The following are standard civil ceremony vows.

(Name), I take you to be my lawfully wedded (husband/wife).

Before these witnesses I vow to love you and care for you as long as we both shall live.

I take you with all your faults and your strengths as I offer myself to you with my faults and my strengths.

I will help you when you need help and will turn to you when I need help.

I choose you as the person with whom I will spend my life.

4

A World of Poems, Blessings, Meditations, and Quotations

To the world you may be one person, but to one person you may be the world.

—BILL WILSON

For many of us expressing our feelings of love is difficult to do, and when we have to do it standing up in front of an audience it may seem quite frightening. This chapter is rich with timeless poems, readings, thoughts, and reflections that may touch your heart and the hearts of others even as they may also stir tears of happiness.

In Washington, writers are often called in to "punch up" a speech with memorable sayings or quotations. Here are some poignant words to "punch up" your vows. You can also use what you are about to read as a boilerplate from which you create your own vows or personal poems. Asking family members or friends to give a reading during the ceremony is a wonderful way to honor their special role in your life as they honor the role love plays in all our lives.

If you find that your tongue is tied, or your pen has run out of inspirational ink, or you simply want to enrich your ceremony with what some of the best and brightest have said about love and marriage over the ages, this chapter contains the stuff to stir the flow of emotions and love. Here you will find brief thoughts on love from sources as varied as the Bible, Mark Twain, Lao-tzu, Mother Teresa, and Katharine Hepburn. Use these quotations as a catalyst to give language to caring or to find your inspiration.

Because many of us discover our spirituality outside of traditional forms or find our religion enriched by a multitude of influences, in these readings and thoughts you may discover ideas, or draw on the words of others, to make your vows your own, your day more spiritually expressive of you.

Poems, Blessings, and Meditations

*Now you will feel no rain, for each of you will be
the shelter for the other. Now you will feel no
cold, for each of you will be the warmth for the
other. Now you are two persons, but there is only
one life before. Go now to your dwelling place to
enter into the days of your life together. And may
your days be good and long upon the earth.*

—APACHE WEDDING BLESSING

*Alone in bed
her image clearly comes—
I can see her long hair,
feel it smooth
to the touch of my palms.*

—FUJIWARA TEIKA, ANCIENT JAPAN

*You are my friend. And a friend is one to whom
one may pour out all the contents of one's heart,
chaff and grain together, knowing that the
gentlest of hands will take and sift it, keep what
is worth keeping and, with the breath of kindness,
blow the rest away.*

—ARABIC BLESSING

O my beautiful one.
Are you not my health and my life?
You are health to the heart that finds you.

—FRAGMENT FROM AN ANCIENT EGYPTIAN LOVE POEM

There is nothing without a cause. The coming
together of this man and woman is not an
accident; it is the foreordained result of numerous
previous lives. This bond cannot be made less or
broken. In the time ahead, this joyous occasion
will arrive as surely as the morning even though
difficult times will arrive as inevitably as the
darkening night sky. When things go joyously,
take the time to meditate. When things cause you
sadness, take the time to meditate. To only say the
words "love and compassion" comes easily. But to
know that love and compassion are dependent on
perseverance and patience is not easy. If you
remember this, your marriage will have strength
and be everlasting.

—ADAPTED BUDDHIST MARRIAGE TEACHING

Your love is from life's great mystery
It lies beneath a great quiet lake . . .
It is like the deep truth of a dark well.

Your love is purity and coolness . . .
You have no need to make waves in the water
You have no need to dig another well
You only have need to watch yourself with clarity
And drink deeply from your love.

—TAO TE CHING, ADAPTED

You left impressions unforgettable
and when I view our moon
your image surfaces
and that love seems forever.

—SAIGYO, ANCIENT JAPAN

Let the earth of my body be mixed with the earth
    my beloved walks on.
Let the fire of my body be the light in the mirror
    that reflects his face.
Let the water of my body combine with the water
    of the lotus pool he bathes in.
Let the breath of my body be air soothing his
    exhausted limbs.
Let me be calm sky over my beloved.

—ADAPTED HINDU LOVE POEM

She is the only girl. There are no others.
She is more beautiful than any other.

She is a star goddess arising.
She has captured my heart.

—EGYPTIAN LOVE POEM FROM A
3,000-YEAR-OLD PAPYRUS

As even the ant brought gifts to Solomon,
So do I bring my soul, my love, to you.

—ADAPTED FRAGMENT FROM A TURKOMAN LOVE SONG

What relation could my mother be
to yours? What relation is my father
to yours? And how
did you and I meet ever?
But in love our hearts are as the red
earth and pouring rain:
mingled
beyond parting.

—TAMIL (INDIA) POEM WRITTEN IN SANSKRIT
2,000 YEARS AGO

My grief has come to an end. Now is the season
of joy. The flowers of Spring are like jewels in my
green garden. Let us walk together through its
paths. Go! Tell the nightingale that Spring is
here.

And tell the poet to come with his lute. Let him sing us a song of the flowers of Spring. I only pray that you do not listen to the parrot whispering to the rose that Autumn will soon arrive.

With Spring my love you have returned to me, and again I gaze on the moon of my great delight. Let us leave it to others to have their festivals. Our only festival is when, in Spring, I can see my love's footsteps through the garden like twin flowers on their toes. And I will be in love's soft arms.

—ADAPTED AFGHAN LOVE SONG

When one has a young woman's love, who would then envy the immortal gods?

—LI TAI PO, EIGHTH-CENTURY CHINA
LOVE POEM FRAGMENT, ADAPTED

May you walk in beauty.
May there be beauty before you.
May there be beauty behind you.
My there be beauty above and below you.

—ESKIMO BLESSING FOR THE EXCHANGE OF VOWS

May you find the strength of an eagle's wings,
And the courage and faith to soar to great heights,
And may you be granted the universal wisdom to
carry you there.

—NAVAJO SONG OF BLESSING AFTER VOWS

There is only one caste, the caste of humanity.
There is only one religion, the religion of love.
There is only one language, the language of the
heart.

—SATHYA SAI BABA

Oh, I am thinking
Oh, I am thinking
I have found my lover
Oh, I am sure it is so.

—CHIPPEWA POEM OF BETROTHAL

My boat is floating on the sky.
And I am also as my beloved is a dream mirrored
on my heart.

—TU FU, EIGHTH-CENTURY CHINA
LOVE POEM FRAGMENT

*I take in as my breath the sweet air that comes
    from you.*
I witness your beauty every day.
*I desire to hear your voice on the north wind each
    day so the strength in my arms may be reborn
    with your love.*
*Call for me through eternity, and I will always be
    there.*

—ADAPTED FROM AN ANCIENT EGYPTIAN TEXT

*The white star at twilight is fair, and the sky
    clears at the day's end,*
*but she is more fair to me, more dear to me, she is
    my heart's friend.*

—TRADITIONAL SHOSHONE LOVE POEM

Let there be peace between neighbors.
Let there be peace between family.
Let there be peace between each of us.
Let there be peace between husband and wife.
Let there be peace in our hearts.

—ADAPTED CELTIC BLESSING

*To love you is like having a luscious fruit ripening
    in my hand,*
Like having dates swimming in my honey wine.

The moment lingers.
The taste lasts.
We will remain joined until the end of years.
We will remain together in the endless line of
    hours.
We shall join together in this taste of bread and
    wine.

—ANCIENT EGYPT, ADAPTED POEM

My love for you is bigger than earth,
and higher than the sky,
more unfathomable than the seas
is this love for this man.

—TAMIL (INDIA) POETRY WRITTEN IN SANSKRIT
2,000 YEARS AGO

From this day forward,
You shall not walk alone.
My heart will be your shelter,
And my arms will be your home.

—AUTHOR UNKNOWN

True love is a sacred flame
That burns eternally,
And none can dim its special glow
Or change its destiny.

True love speaks in tender tones
And hears with gentle ear,
True love gives with open heart
And true love conquers fear.
True love makes no harsh demands,
It neither rules nor binds,
And true love holds with gentle hands
The hearts that it entwines.

—AUTHOR UNKNOWN

I know not whether thou has been absent:
I lie down with thee, I rise up with thee,
In my dreams thou art with me.
If my eardrops tremble in my ears,
I know it is thou moving within my heart.

—AZTEC WEDDING PRAYER

The Confirmation

Yes, yours, my love, is the right human face.
I in my mind had waited for this long,
Seeing the false and searching for the true,
Then found you as a traveler finds a place
Of welcome suddenly amid the wrong
Valleys and rocks and twisting roads. But you,

[101]

What shall I call you? A fountain in a waste,
A well of water in a country dry,
Or anything that's honest and good, an eye
That makes the whole world bright. Your open
    heart,
Simple with giving, gives the primal deed,
The first good world, the blossom, the blowing
    seed,
The hearth, the steadfast land, the wandering sea.
Not beautiful or rare in every part,
But like yourself, as they were meant to be.

                         —EDWIN MUIR

These I Can Promise

I cannot promise you a life of sunshine;
I cannot promise riches, wealth, or gold;
I cannot promise you an easy pathway
That leads away from change or growing old.
But I can promise all my heart's devotion;
A smile to chase away your tears of sorrow;
A love that's ever true and ever growing;
A hand to hold in yours through each tomorrow.

                         —AUTHOR UNKNOWN

*Then Almitra spoke again and said, And what of
   Marriage, Master?*
And he answered saying:
*You were born together, and together you shall be
   forevermore.*
*You shall be together when the white wings of
   death scatter your days.*
*Ay, you shall be together even in the silent
   memory of God.*
But let there be spaces in your togetherness,
*And let the winds of the heavens dance between
   you.*
Love one another, but make not a bond of love:
*Let it rather be a moving sea between the shores
   of your souls.*
Fill each other's cup but drink not from one cup.
*Give one another of your bread but eat not from
   the same loaf.*
*Sing and dance together and be joyous, but let
   each one of you be alone,*
*Even as the strings of a lute are alone though
   they quiver with the same music.*
*Give your hearts, but not into each other's
   keeping.*
For only the hand of Life can contain your hearts.

And stand together yet not too near together:
For the pillars of the temple stand apart,
And the oak tree and the cypress grow not in each
    other's shadow.

—EXCERPT FROM THE PROPHET

You have become mine forever.
Yes, we have become partners.
I have become yours.
Hereafter, I cannot live without you.
Do not live without me.
Let us share the joys.
We are word and meaning, united.
You are thought and I am sound.

—KAHLIL GIBRAN

May the nights be honey-sweet for us.
May the mornings be honey-sweet for us.
May the plants be honey-sweet for us.
May the earth be honey-sweet for us.

—HINDU MARRIAGE POEM

May the road rise to meet you,
May the wind be always at your back,
May the sun shine warm upon your face,
The rains fall soft upon your fields,

And until we meet again,
May God hold you in the palm of his hand.
May God be with you and bless you;
May you see your children's children.
May you be poor in misfortune,
Rich in blessings.
May you know nothing but happiness
From this day forward.
May the road rise to meet you,
May the wind be always at your back,
May the warm rays of sun fall upon your home,
And may the hand of a friend always be near.
May green be the grass you walk on,
May blue be the skies above you,
May pure be the joys that surround you,
May true be the hearts that love you.

—IRISH BLESSINGS

When two people are at one
in their inmost hearts,
they shatter even the strength of iron or bronze.
And when two people understand each other
in their inmost hearts,
their words are sweet and strong,
like the fragrance of orchids.

—EXCERPT FROM THE *I CHING*

God in heaven above please protect the ones we
    love.
We honor all you created as we pledge our hearts
    and lives together.
We honor mother-earth—and ask for our marriage
    to be abundant and grow stronger through the
    seasons;
We honor fire—and ask that our union be warm
    and glowing with love in our hearts;
We honor wind—and ask we sail though life safe
    and calm as in our father's arms;
We honor water—to clean and soothe our
    relationship that it may never thirst for love;
With all the forces of the universe you created, we
    pray for harmony and true happiness as we
    forever grow young together. Amen.

—CHEROKEE PRAYER

Well, when one happens on his own particular
half, the two of them are wondrously thrilled with
affection and intimacy and love, and are hardly to
be induced to leave each other's side for a single
moment. These are they who continue together
throughout life. No one could imagine this to be
the mere amorous connection: obviously the soul
of each is wishing for something else that it

cannot express. Suppose that Hephaestus should ask, "Do you desire to be joined in the closest possible union, that so long as you live, the pair of you, being as one, may share a single life?" Each would unreservedly deem that he had been offered just what he was yearning for all the time.

—PLATO, FROM *THE SYMPOSIUM*

Thoughts on Love and Marriage

Love conquers all things; let us too surrender to love.

—VIRGIL

If love were what the rose is, and I were like the leaf, our lives would grow together in sad or singing weather.

—ALGERNON CHARLES SWINBURNE

Whither thou goest, I will go; and where thou lodgest, I will lodge; thy people shall be my people, and thy God, my God.

—BOOK OF RUTH, 1:16–17

To make One, there must be Two.

—W. H. AUDEN

Love is the joy of the good, the wonder of the wise, the amazement of the Gods.

—PLATO

Love is a fruit in season at all times, and within the reach of every hand.

—MOTHER TERESA

By all means marry. If you get a good wife you will be very happy; if you get a bad one you will become a philosopher—and that is good for any man.

—SOCRATES

What greater thing is there for two human souls than to feel that they are joined together to strengthen each other in all labor, to minister to each other in all sorrow, to share with each other in all gladness, to be one with each other in the silent unspoken memories?

—GEORGE ELIOT

*In marriage, every day you love, and every day
you forgive. It is an ongoing sacrament, love and
forgiveness.*

—BILL MOYERS

Two hearts that beat as one.

—JOHN KEATS

*Love has nothing to do with what you are
expecting to get—only what you are expecting to
give, which is everything. What you will receive in
return varies. But it really has no connection with
what you give. You give because you love and
cannot help giving. If you are very lucky, you may
be loved back.*

—KATHARINE HEPBURN

*There is no fear in love, but perfect love casteth
out fear.*

—1 JOHN 4:18

*It is easy to love people far away. It is not always
easy to love those close to us. It is easier to give a
cup of rice to relieve hunger than to relieve the*

*loneliness and pain of someone unloved in our
own home. Bring love into your home, for this is
where our love for each other must start.*

—MOTHER TERESA

*The best portion of a good man's life,
His little, nameless, unremembered acts,
Of kindness and of love.*

—WILLIAM WORDSWORTH

*When you fish for love, bait with your heart, not
your brain.*

—MARK TWAIN

*A good marriage is that in which each appoints
the other guardian of his solitude.*

—RAINER MARIA RILKE

There is no remedy for love but to love more.

—HENRY DAVID THOREAU

We are shaped and fashioned by what we love.

—GOETHE

To keep your marriage brimming,
With love in the loving cup,
Whenever you're wrong, admit it;
Whenever you're right, shut up.

—OGDEN NASH

Grow old along with me; the best is yet to be.

—ROBERT BROWNING

Immature love says, "I love you because I need
   you."
Mature love says, "I need you because I love you."

—ERICH FROMM

Life has taught me that love does not consist of
gazing at each other but looking outward together
in the same direction.

—ANTOINE DE SAINT-EXUPERY

Till I loved I never lived—enough.

—EMILY DICKINSON

What a grand thing to be loved.
What a grander thing still to love.

—VICTOR HUGO

Kindness in words creates confidence.
Kindness in thought creates profoundness.
Kindness in giving creates love.

—LAO-TZU

He who is in love is wise and is becoming wiser,
sees newly every time he looks at the object
beloved, drawing from it with his eyes and his
mind those virtues which it possesses.

—RALPH WALDO EMERSON

All things to their destruction do draw,
Only our love hath no decay;
This, no tomorrow hath, no yesterday.

—JOHN DONNE

And now here is my secret, a very simple secret; it
is only with the heart that one can see rightly,
what is essential is invisible to the eye.

—ANTOINE DE SAINT-EXUPERY

5

A World of Proverbs

Union gives strength.

—AESOP

No matter the tradition you or your lover were raised with, tradition is in each of our lives and enriches our lives. This chapter contains delightful proverbs you may want to keep in mind when crafting your wedding vows or other elements of your ceremony. Even if you don't incorporate these into your ceremony, you'll no doubt benefit from contemplating the messages and thoughts contained in them. No matter where you or your family live or came from, the following selection offers a few words of wisdom—and a few laughs—from the ages.

In a world spinning faster and faster, adding tradition to your vows may make the magic moment linger and your special moment more special.

Take what serves you. Be enriched by all.

Marriage is not a race; you can always get there on time.

—RUSSIAN PROVERB

He who marries might be sorry; he who does not will be sorry.

—CZECH PROVERB

The best minister in life is the human heart; the best teacher is time; the best friend is God.

—YIDDISH PROVERB

Marriage is a game best played by two winners.

—AMERICAN PROVERB

There may be snow on the roof, but there is still a fire in the chimney.

—ENGLISH PROVERB

An old love does not rust.

—RUSSIAN PROVERB

He that falls in love with himself will have no rivals.

—AMERICAN PROVERB

Forced love does not last.

—DUTCH PROVERB

It is easy to reconcile when there is love.

—WELSH PROVERB

A man too good for the world is not good to his wife.

—YIDDISH PROVERB

If love interferes with your business, quit your business.

—AMERICAN PROVERB

Love, a cough, and poverty will not remain a secret.

—YIDDISH PROVERB

Love and blindness are twin sisters.

—RUSSIAN PROVERB

*Love and foolishness differ from each other only
in name.*

> —HUNGARIAN PROVERB

Choose your love and then love your choice.

> —AMERICAN PROVERB

*Love, like rain, does not choose the grass on
which it falls.*

> —ZULU PROVERB

*Love enters man through his eyes; a woman
through her ears.*

> —POLISH PROVERB

*In love affairs there comes a moment when desire
demands possession.*

> —YIDDISH PROVERB

*Love has made heroes of many and fools of many
more.*

> —SWEDISH PROVERB

Love at first sight is cured by a second look.

> —AMERICAN PROVERB

Love is a ring, and a ring has no end.

—RUSSIAN PROVERB

The loneliest person is someone who loves only himself.

—YIDDISH PROVERB

Love is sweet torment.

—ENGLISH PROVERB

Love is all-important, and it is its own reward.

—TAMIL PROVERB

Marriage and cooking call for forethought.

—GREEK PROVERB

It is better to marry a quiet fool than a witty scold.

—ENGLISH PROVERB

Married today, married tomorrow.

—FRENCH PROVERB

To love and be wise is impossible.

—AMERICAN PROVERB

Love never dies of starvation, but often of indigestion.

—AMERICAN PROVERB

One cannot be a lover by force.

—TURKISH PROVERB

Love takes away the sight, and matrimony restores it.

—AMERICAN PROVERB

Early marriage, long love.

—GERMAN PROVERB

He who loves a thing often talks of it.

—EGYPTIAN PROVERB

Whom we love best, to them we can often say little.

—ENGLISH PROVERB

Puppy love can lead to a dog's life.

—AMERICAN PROVERB

Let him not be a lover who has no courage.

—ITALIAN PROVERB

It is better to love someone you cannot have than to have someone you cannot love.

—AMERICAN PROVERB

Lovers always think that others are blind.

—ITALIAN PROVERB

Where there's no love, all faults are seen.

—GERMAN PROVERB

Better love me little, but love me long.

—YIDDISH PROVERB

Love is strongest in pursuit—marriage in possession.

—AMERICAN PROVERB

If more people tried as hard to stay married as they do to get married, fewer marriages would go on the rocks.

—AMERICAN PROVERB

Love rules its kingdom without a sword.

—ENGLISH PROVERB

Love will creep where it cannot go.

—ENGLISH PROVERB

Even when it rains, old and true love never rusts.

—HEBREW PROVERB

There's always room for love in a budget.

—ENGLISH PROVERB

Love makes men orators.

—ENGLISH PROVERB

Love makes time pass away, but too often time makes love pass away.

—FRENCH PROVERB

Love or a fire in your trousers is not easy to conceal.

—SWEDISH PROVERB

Love is an excuse for its own faults.

—ITALIAN PROVERB

Love knows hidden paths. All the hidden paths.

—GERMAN PROVERB

Love laughs at locksmiths.

—ENGLISH PROVERB

Love levels all inequalities.

—ITALIAN PROVERB

Love looks for love again.

—ENGLISH PROVERB

Love is never without jealousy.

—SCOTTISH PROVERB

Love cannot dwell with suspicion.

—AMERICAN PROVERB

Love is never without some thorns.

—SLOVAKIAN PROVERB

Love is not an impartial judge.

—IRISH PROVERB

Love is shown by deeds, not by words.

—PHILIPPINE PROVERB

Love is the true price of love.

—ENGLISH PROVERB

Love is like butter—it's good with bread.

—YIDDISH PROVERB

Love is like fog; there is no mountain on which it does not rest.

—HAWAIIAN PROVERB

Love is the master of all arts.

—ITALIAN PROVERB

Wedding Symbols, Traditions, and Superstitions

*Love is an irresistible desire to be
irresistibly desired.*

—ROBERT FROST

*I*n this chapter you will find a collection of the symbols, traditions, and superstitions of love and marriage. They are as varied and interesting as the countries and cultures that gave birth to them. Part folk, part fun, and part poking fun, these nuggets have survived the test of time to give you a bit of laughter and levity just when you need it most.

Incorporate them into your wedding day and see if they still hold up, or share them with your honey to remind each other that, while you may be a bit crazy right now, you aren't *that* crazy!

Have fun with these old customs and superstitions. Be a bit devilish and spring one on your groom or bride. Or, use some of the more touching ones to include your parents, friends, or other family members into the meaning of the day. Whether you decide to court good luck by getting married under a full moon, having the groom walk around the bride seven times, or asking the best man to walk into your new home backward, we wish you good luck on your very special day. And if it rains on your wedding day, don't forget—that's very good luck!

Giving the Bride Away

Many years ago a woman was considered to belong to her father, therefore when she married it was her father who "gave her away" to the groom to become his responsibility. Sometimes the groom was given a pair of the bride's old shoes as a sign that it was now his duty to provide shoes for her. This represented the passing of responsibility for pleasing the bride from the father to the groom.

In some instances the groom would hold the bride on his left arm when he kidnapped her, leaving his right arm, the sword arm, available to fight off any other suitors. This is the reason that the groom usually stands on the bride's right side during the wedding ceremony. During the kidnapping if the groom needed assistance, he would ask his best friend to be his best man. This of course led to the tradition of the groom having a best man during the wedding ceremony.

Because a marriage used to be looked at as a way to bring together opposing families, the families of the groom and bride would sit on opposite sides of the aisle during the ceremony to try to avoid any arguing.

Something Old, Something New . . .

Just about all brides have heard the phrase, "something old, something new, something borrowed, something blue, a shiny penny in her shoe." But where did all this come from, and what is the meaning?

Here is the simple breakdown: Wearing something old adds something from the bride's past life to her new life and ensures continuity. Something new reflects her acceptance of her new life. Something borrowed — a symbol from a woman the bride is close with, who has a strong and happy marriage, to support in lasting marital bliss — reflects that none of us is alone, we are all a part of a family or a community. And something blue reflects what blue has long reflected in literature — love, fidelity, and purity. As far as a shiny penny is concerned, maybe at one time it was so you could always call home . . . or to ensure future prosperity.

If the bride brings something borrowed on her honeymoon she will also be bringing good luck.

If the bride gives her love a penny before the marriage ceremony, the couple will always have money.

The Wedding Ring

The custom of wearing wedding rings comes from ancient times. The ancient Egyptians believed that the circular shape of the ring symbolized an eternity of love, a love that had no beginning or end. The third finger on the left hand was the chosen finger to wear the wedding ring because since the ancient Egyptians and Romans it has been believed that a vein runs from the fourth finger of the left hand straight to the heart. It was also believed that the wearing of the ring kept love from escaping from the heart.

The engagement ring was originally used as a way to show the community that the woman had been "sold" by her father to her soon-to-be husband. The engagement ring was many times gold as a sign representing the groom's worth.

There is also a long-held belief that the groom should make a wish when he puts the ring on his bride's hand, and vice versa.

Flowers

Flowers are a beautiful accent to the wedding ceremony. You may wish to choose flowers by their symbolic meaning. A few examples follow:

Lilacs and roses signify love.

Freesias stand for friendship.

Lilies represent purity.

Chrysanthemums are a symbol of truth.

Ferns represent sincerity.

Heather is thought to bring good luck.

Gypsophila is associated with fertility.

Ivy signifies a long-lasting marriage.

Myrtle is associated with Venus, the goddess of love.

In medieval times the bride's bouquet was traditionally composed of chives, garlic, rosemary, bay leaves, and assorted other strong-smelling herbs and flowers to dispel evil spirits.

Hawaiian brides wear seven strands of pikaki flowers in order to assure good luck.

During the sixteenth century, in Elizabethan times, both the bride and groom carried bouquets of rosemary, which to Elizabethans represented remembrance. Often, twentieth-century brides in North America carried rosemary bouquets to symbolize virginity and innocence and induce fidelity.

Rosemary is also used to bedeck the wedding bed, and in some communities the bridesmaids still give the groom rosemary as well. Ironically, in old apothecary manuals, rosemary is often depicted as a contraceptive.

During the reception, the bride throws her bouquet over her shoulder to the single female guests. It is the tradition that the woman who catches the bouquet will be the next to marry.

What Color Dress?

The tradition of wearing a white bridal gown started when Queen Victoria wore white in her wedding to symbolize her virginity. It is also tradition that the bride's wedding dress should not be made by her and that she should not be seen in her wedding dress by the groom before the ceremony.

The tradition for the bridesmaids to dress as beautifully as the bride was to puzzle evil spirits who might be trying to catch the bride. The custom of the bride wearing a veil came from the Romans, also as a way to camouflage the bride from evil spirits and to keep her safe. However, Victorian brides wore a veil to represent respect, virginity, and modesty.

Across time in Western cultures, wedding gowns have traditionally been either white or blue because in tradition and literature, white represents purity and innocence while blue symbolizes fidelity and honest love.

In Islamic cultures, brides wear red wedding gowns symbolizing the color of blood and the life force. Eastern European brides often wear red veils.

Shoes

If you put honey on the sole of your shoes you will have a sweet life.

It's good luck to get married in old shoes.

If you write the name of your unmarried friends on your shoes, the first name to rub off when you walk down the aisle will be the next one married.

According to a German and Russian tradition a bride who wears a piece of palm in her shoe the night before the wedding will have luck in her marriage.

And this I am sure you did not know: if you put salt and dill in both the bride's and groom's shoes they will be protected from witchcraft.

Throw shoes after the bride and groom because this means they will always have clothes . . . well, certainly shoes.

First Vows

The groom states his vow for the marriage first as a way to symbolize his being the initiator of the relationship and assuming the greatest responsibility in the marriage.

Bachelor and Bachelorette Parties

The bachelor party originated from what was called "stag night," which started as a way to ward off evil spirits before the wedding. The bachelorette party was originally called "hen night" in Anglo-Saxon traditions. However, in this day and age both events tend to involve a party in commemoration of being single, ranging from a wild night in Las Vegas to a girls' weekend of spa treatment.

The Kiss

In a very pleasant tradition, the bride must be kissed in order for her marriage to be lucky, and the groom must be the first person to kiss her.

Everyone at the wedding must kiss the bride in order for her to be lucky.

When you kiss a bride you will find you have again found firm footing with someone you recently argued with.

Ensuring Good Luck

There is a tradition that suggests if the best man walks backward into the bride and groom's new home it is good luck.

Custom has it that if neither the bride nor the groom sweeps the floor in their new home for seven days after their wedding, it will bring good luck.

While it is considered good luck to give a bride and groom a fork, if a friend gives a knife it is bad luck, and the receiver of the gift must give the giver a penny or the knife will cut into their friendship.

It has long been considered good luck to marry on the groom's birthday, but bad luck to marry on the bride's.

Full Moon

If you get married under a full moon or when the moon is waxing, your happiness will increase and increase. If you get married under a full moon, you and your spouse will have full lives, full pockets, and full hearts.

When to Marry

Throughout time, June has been a popular month for weddings. One reason is because June was the month of Juno, the queen of the gods and the goddess of marriage. June also has the longest day of the year, which people have always thought meant the couple would have a long and happy life together.

November marriages are thought to have great fortune, December marriages increasing love, and July weddings promise a sweet, sweet life to always remember.

Let It Rain

If it rains on the wedding day, the bride will never need to shed tears herself.

Rain falling on the bridal veil is a sign of good fortune.

Rain falling on the bride is a rain of good wishes washing away any troubles the couple may encounter.

But to ensure good luck, be sure to keep your feet dry on your wedding day.

With This Riddle, I Thee Wed

It is an ancient Welsh custom for the bride's father to pose a series of riddles to the groom when he comes to take his bride to the church. And he doesn't offer hints!

Tears

If either the bride or groom cry on their wedding day they will have a long marriage.

In a tradition brought by the Dutch to America, the bride's friend gives the bride a very special handkerchief that she is to carry on her wedding day to catch her tears. Later, the bride gives the handkerchief to her eldest daughter to ensure her good luck.

The Groom's Role

Before the wedding the groom should walk around the bride seven times for luck.

The groom should not carry a wallet on the day he marries, or he'll have no money.

The groom should have a lock of the bride's hair—or, in another tradition, a clove of garlic—in his pocket to ward off evil spirits.

Cake and Other Delicacies

The wedding guests should make a wish while the bride cuts the cake, and their wish will come true.

Three hundred years ago in England someone came up with the idea of putting a piece of wedding cake on your pillow so you would dream of your future spouse. There is an amendment to this tradition, however, that says that it is only the dream you have on the fourth night that comes true. And some people believe that if you sleep on your own cake you will have happiness and good luck.

In the oldest wedding ritual known, the couple shared some food and reflected that they would share their lives together.

A while ago (and a long while ago one assumes) in Russia, the bride and groom were given boiled bear testicles to ensure fertility.

Tossing Rice

Tossing rice after the newlyweds has long been held to ensure fertility and good things growing in their new life together. This is a tradition embraced around the world — except in Sicily, where they toss both barley for male children and wheat for female children. Gypsies traditionally tossed almond blossoms over the bride and groom for luck.

While the wedding guests throw rice on the couple, the couple should themselves throw salt over their left shoulders if they want to add to their good luck.

For the last few hundred years there has been a tradition in England that in addition to rice being thrown, the pathway the bride and groom take should be strewn with objects that show the groom's way of making a living. So if the groom is a tailor there would be pieces of material strewn about. If the groom is a florist there would be flowers. If the groom is a carpenter there would be sawdust and chips of wood. And if the groom is a banker, there would be money . . . just kiddin'.

Symbolic Bread

In many Eastern European traditions the bride, or anyone moving into a new home, is brought salt, a candle, and a piece of bread. This ensures that her life will have spice, light, and plenty.

In some cultures in the Middle East, the bride will put a piece of raw dough at her doorstep as she enters, in the hope that the rising dough will be reflected in her hopes for becoming pregnant.

The night before the wedding the bride and groom should share a piece of bread with honey to ensure them of a sweet life together.

Children

If you put an ax under the bed, you are assured of having a male child.

If a flock of birds fly over the bride's car on the way to be married, this means you are going to have many children. If you can count how many birds, you are also supposed to discover how many children.

If the bride sits on a piece of lamb's wool while wearing her wedding dress, she will have children with wavy hair.

If the bride and groom are both wearing untied shoes, or perhaps loafers, when they marry, childbirth will be easy.

Giving birth is facilitated if the mom wears the gloves (snow mittens don't count) she wore at her wedding.

Breaking Glass

In a Germanic tradition people show up at the bride's home the night before the wedding and break dishes on her doorstep to chase away evil spirits.

Other cultures gather up any cracked or chipped dishes and glasses and toss them out the window the night before the wedding so the marriage will not be broken.

In a Jewish wedding, the breaking of a glass at the ceremony's conclusion can represent several things: a memory of the destruction of the ancient Temple in Jerusalem, that the couple will have as many years as there are splinters of glass, or the breaking with their past single lives and the beginning of their new lives together.

While Greeks are generally big on breaking plates for almost any happy occasion, Greek traditions have people breaking champagne glasses on the wedding night for luck and long life together.

In England, some brides take a plate with their cake on it and drop it from the top of their house for good luck.

And in gypsy cultures the father of the bride and groom together break a pot and try to read how many grandchildren there will be from the number of shards.

And if you accidentally break a glass on your wedding day, don't worry, this also is a tradition of good luck.

More Good Fortune, Good Luck, Good Life Together

If you get married at home, make sure to leave by the front door for good luck.

It's lucky to have an even number of wedding guests.

The bride should not drive on her wedding day if she wants good luck.

In your marriage, if you sleep facing north, you will always be happy. If you sleep facing the rising sun you will always be healthy. And if you sleep facing each other your marriage will be peaceful.

Afterword

At the end of your very special day, you and your love will find yourselves at the beginning of the rest of your lives together. Sometimes it can be hard to remember that amid all the wedding planning something more wonderful is yet to come. And we hope that we have been friends—even at a distance—and allies in your efforts to make your vows very WOW.

As we prepared this book, our editors suggested that we write a brief afterword. It is both curious and telling that while we worked on this separately, we both wrote something that spoke to the same issue—the heart. Clearly we thought that this last piece of advice was at the heart of anything and everything in life and in you and your beloved's life together.

So, this is from Jordan: When I was in school, one of my best friends had this quote on his school notebook, and it has stuck with me ever since. Maybe it will stick with you:

> *I have learned that the head does not hear*
> *anything until the heart has listened, and what*
> *the heart knows today, the head will understand*
> *tomorrow.*

And this is from Noah: In my life I have come to learn that my heart knows what my mind only thinks it knows.

And this is from both of us: Congratulations. Together, may you follow the path with a heart.

About the Authors

Noah benShea is a poet, philosopher, scholar, humorist, and international bestselling author. His books on Jacob the Baker are embraced around the world and have influenced generations. He has been an assistant dean at UCLA, a fellow at esteemed think tanks, and his work has been included in publications of Oxford University and the World Bible Society in Jerusalem. His weekly inspirational essay, "Noah's Window," has been carried nationally via the *New York Times* Regional Syndicate and was nominated for a Pulitzer Prize. Mr. benShea's recent book *Remember This My Children* was a finalist for Gift Book of the Year. He is a frequent keynote lecturer who has spoken at the Library of Congress as well as to educators, business, and community leaders across North America. Widely interviewed on radio and television, Mr. benShea has two children, lives in Santa Barbara, California, and actually reads the mail at his website, noahswindow.com.

Jordan benShea grew up in Santa Barbara, California. She attended high school in Santa Barbara and England and graduated from the University of California at Berkeley with a double major in mass communications and business administration. Ms. benShea has subsequently held positions in finance, marketing, and business development in Los Angeles. She is currently in product marketing management for a leading company in the biometrics industry. It is her lifelong fascination with weddings that sparked her curiosity and commitment to this book. When not working on her next book, Ms. benShea can be found at the beach reading, running, or hiking the Montecito hills near her childhood home.